The Lily of the Valley

"More Inspiration for the Soul"

"From my Heart to your Heart"

DEDICATION

This book is written with much love for my Lord and Savior Jesus Christ and for my precious family. My husband Bill, and three wonderful children, Debbie, Karen and Mark, along with my grandchildren Michael, Russell, Rita, Christopher, and Courtney who are all my special gifts from God.

I wish I had the time and space to mention all the people that have been added to my life over the last forty years. The Lord has truly blessed me with a wonderful circle of friends, that I will have throughout Eternity, and some I spoke about in my first book, "Reflections of His Love", and now, with the release of "The Lily of the Valley", I not only dedicate this offering to my family but to some dear friends as well.

Ruby Joann Kolajajck, my dear sister-in-Christ, has been a friend for the last fifteen years, and she never fails to call just when I'm having a bad day or I'm in need of prayer for some reason. We both enjoy going to prison together, or should I say, going on our Bill Glass, Champions for Life, prison weekends? We always share a room, and the time spent together and with the inmates is and has always been one of the greatest high-points in my life. We have some awesome times in prisons all over the United States and Mexico. I love you, dear One. Thanks for your continued support and encouragement regarding the writing of both books. You'll always be the sister I never had.

The Lord moved Bill and me to Atlanta, Georgia five years ago and He assigned us a spot on Fountain Lakes Dr. in Lawrenceville. And what a great joy it has been living across the street from my dear friend Sharon, her husband, Art and her mother, Faith. They have truly been a great blessing and a very gracious gift from my Father. I can honestly say it's been so much fun being able to run back and forth across the street at any hour of the day or night. I couldn't have had more wonderful neighbors if I could have looked all over the world and hand-picked them myself. Thank you, Lord for my dear friends.

My great, faithful friends, Tom and Adrienne, just a super blessing and Tom is also in prison ministry with me and Joann, so quite frequently the three of us travel together. The Lord introduced us at church, and they were the first friends He gave us upon arriving in Atlanta. Adrienne was such a blessing, helping me to shop for furniture. We've spent every holiday together for the last five years for we're all four far from our families.

My precious Robert in San Antonio who is like an adopted son and he is truly a great blessing to my life. Renna in Dallas who has been like a daughter to me from the day we met in a very unusual place and in a unique way. I thank God for you.

My dear friends, named and unnamed, what can I ever say to let you know what you mean to me, and please, know that I thank my God upon every remembrance of you.

To God be the Glory!

Contents

INTRODUCTION

"The Lily of the Valley" is a book of Christian poems and devotionals written following my first book, "Reflections of His Love". After completing Reflections I started to go back and edit all the poems to make sure they were correct in rhyme and meter and meeting all the poetic criteria for perfection. I started going over the original writings, and suddenly I felt strongly that I should have them published exactly as the Holy Spirit laid them on my heart. I do want my readers to know that everything that I have ever written the Lord not only gave me to speak to others but each poem or story speaks to me as well.

If I had gone ahead and made changes in what the Lord gave me in the first book, I honestly don't believe I would have been given poems and commentaries for "The Lily of the Valley". The poems in both books will hopefully, bless, instruct, uplift, convict, encourage, enlighten or simply minister to some need in the reader's life; but above all my prayer is, that in some way they will bring honor, glory and praise to my wonderful Father God and my precious Savior, the Lord Jesus Christ.

If anyone reads this book and then gives their life to Christ; and they change their final destination from hell for Eternity to Heaven, then I of all people am most blessed. I am truly humbled that the Lord would give me the privilege of serving Him in any way, and all my love and thanksgiving go to Him.

May the Lord richly bless you as you read this book and as you in turn seek to serve Him.

To God be the glory!

The Lily of the Valley

Dear One, what a wonderful Father God we have. If you've ever found yourself at a loss for words, then you can understand what I'm about to say. There are times when I simply feel like praising the Lord, because He is so wonderful; and yet it seems that too soon I find myself speechless and unable to express myself. It's as if there aren't enough words in the dictionary to truly describe our God. When I think of His character, all that He really is and that He so lovingly does for His children; it's totally beyond our ability to communicate with our limited vocabulary.

It is such a blessing to take a few minutes just to meditate on our Father and how richly He has blessed us. If you've never done it, take a pen and paper and write down everything that comes to your mind, when you stop and think about the Lord, and who He is and how He has blessed you. I believe you'll find that you just might run out of paper, if not I'm sure you'll run out of words, just as I have.

The Lord is so much more and so much greater, than any mere words - we can conjure up to describe Him and praise Him - could ever effectively convey. I highly recommend taking the time to praise Him regularly, for when you do it will glorify Him and bless you, as well. Besides, do it, if for no other reason, simply because He's worth it! Isn't He?

Read Psalms chapter 34 and then focus on verse 1: His praise will always be on my lips.

Read Psalms chapter 63 and then focus on verse 4: I will praise you as long as I live.

Read at least one chapter of Psalms and one of Proverbs daily for it is the - Medicine for the soul.
Enjoy, Enjoy, Enjoy it!

The Lily of the Valley

He's the Lily of the Valley,
The Bright and Morning Star,
He's the sweetest Rose of Sharon,
Most Beautiful by far.

He's the God of Grace and Glory
The Way, the Truth, the Life,
He will calm your deepest fears and
Remove your sin and strife.

He's Creator and Sustainer
Your Father and Best Friend,
He would never ever leave you...
He'll be with you to the end.

He's Light that shines in the Darkness...
So you can find your way
He heals the brokenhearted and
Then turns their night to day.

He said, "When you feel alone just
Call out and I'll be there.
Although others may forsake you
You know I wouldn't dare.

Make My Word Your compass...it's not...
Simply another book;
It will quickly ease your pain
If you'll just take a look.

All your friends may walk away but...
You can depend on me,
I'll make the lame to walk again
And cause the blind to see.

I'm all that you'll ever need and
Leave you - I would never,
I'll be with you for Eternity
That's infinitely forever.

Pray

Friend, it's not that we don't love the Lord, is it? It's simply that life sometimes gets in our way. We have good intentions, but something always seems to come up to interfere with our prayer life.

There are some Christians that only pray when they're in trouble or when they need something. Some pray when they're afraid or when they've lost their way.

The Word of God tells us that we should pray without ceasing. Prayer is talking, communing and fellowshipping with our Heavenly Father, our Spiritual Daddy. He loves to hear from us, in the good times and the bad, the happy times and the sad and whether things are really great or when they're in the pits. He likes to hear from His kids at any time.

We can talk to God in the shower, in the bed, driving down the road(I like to talk to Him out loud - so people probably think I'm singing with the radio or talking on the phone), on our knees, sitting or standing, morning, noon or night. The important thing is to pray and to do it when we're in fellowship, - for it says in Psalms 66:18 If I regard iniquity in my heart He will not hear me - so, it is imperative that we pray with all our known sins confessed.

Dear One, think about one thing, and that is, how would we feel if our spouse or children or anyone we love only talked to us when they wanted or needed something from us. Or what if they didn't speak to us at all for long periods of time, how would we feel? Surely we love the Lord, the One who loves us more than anything and meets our every need, enough to talk to Him daily, if not throughout the day?

Let's all get our priorities in order and put prayer and reading the Word at the top of our list. Prayer is our talking to God and when we read the Word, we're letting the Lord talk back to us, so it's not a one-way conversation.

Read I Thessalonians chapter 5 and then focus on verses 16 - 22: Rejoice in the Lord always, pray without ceasing, in everything give thanks for this is the will of God in Christ Jesus concerning you. Quench not the Spirit, despise not prophesying, test everything, hold fast that which is good and abstain from all appearance of evil.

Read Psalms chapter 32 and then focus on verse 6: Let everyone who is godly pray.

Pray

Pray...when life seems calm and peaceful
Everywhere you go;
As if you're in the forest with...
...Birds singing soft and low.

Pray, when you're having no pain and
When there is no sorrow,
Then at the close of day you can
Look forward to tomorrow.

Pray, when the day skies are blue and
Night's stars are clearly seen,
You're feeling completely at peace
And life seems so serene.

You must pray when darkness dims the skies
Storm clouds begin to roll,
When the battle starts to rage and
There's torment in your soul.

Pray and remember, God still reigns from
His mighty throne on high,
And his loving arm is never too short
To reach us from the sky.

Prayer can pierce through the deepest gloom
Bring light from heaven above;
It can wind its way up to glory and
Come back with God's own love.

Pray to the Father in Jesus' name;
He has all your battles won.
If you don't pray, then remember,
That the war has just begun.

The Image

Why is it, my friend, that for some reason, many Christians, seem to live more than one life? In fact, there are those who even appear to live multiple lives. And yet, a believer needs to be for real, someone others can depend on.

So often, people are one person in their home, in front of their spouse and children, another at their place of employment, still another out with friends, and last but not least, another at church.

There are some who are elders in their church, where everyone in the congregation believes they are the ultimate Christian, and yet at home they are a tyrant and would never think of applying the Word to the relationship they have with their family. Actually, shouldn't our family relationship be second only to the one we have with our Heavenly Father?

Some people are so pious at church and yet tend to make a fool of themselves at sporting events or when out with their friends; and sometimes even at their own children's ballgames and practices. At times, parents can be quite obnoxious and embarrassing for their youngsters. Tragic, when they like to be known as (and called) Christians.

Have you ever had a boss or co-worker who was loud, overbearing and liked to intimidate people? One who liked to make sure everyone knew they were a Christian. Perhaps you had one who even cheated customers and wanted the employees to do the same thing.

It is so important, if we want to be known as a Christian, that we live what we believe. We have to walk the talk and apply God's Word to every area of our lives.

The Lord created us to live a life that honors and glorifies Him. In order to be for real we should let the Lord fill us up and live and minister through us, for that's the one and only way to live a life that pleases Him and blesses others consistently.

Read Matthew Chapter 6 (entire chapter) and focus on verse 33: But seek FIRST His kingdom and His righteousness, and all these other things shall be given to you as well.

The Image

It seems we can't be satisfied with...
What we were meant to be,
So, we try to portray an image...
That we want people to see.

Our Father made us perfectly...
According to His plan,
Why can't we trust that He knew best...
...Since He created man?

Our friends have one image of us...
Family has another;
Can't we be the same for both...
The one and the other?

If someone took a camera and...
Followed us as we roam,
Would they see the same person...
...At work, at church and home?

We won't need to create an image
If we're walking in God's Spirit,
In fact, if we get criticized...
We won't even hear it.

Yes, we need to be the same...
...Wherever we happen to be;
For the Lord knew what He wanted,
When He made you and me...

...But if we live two different lives,
How will people know what's real
You may be one who doesn't care,
And thinks it's no big deal.

But what's not real is just a lie...
So let's...not be image makers,
But start life anew right now by
Being image breakers.

Autumn's in Heaven

Autumn, my precious young niece went home to be with the Lord, totally unexpectedly and in a very tragic manner from the world's perspective. I am including a short story that truly doesn't do her or her wonderful family justice, but hopefully it will give the reader of the poem and the story some incite into the character of this fine young girl and how her life touched and changed others and how it must have blessed and glorified the Lord.

———————

Sixteen years ago, in fact seventeen this December, a precious baby girl was born in the town of Saluda, South Carolina. Terry and Russell, the parents of this beautiful baby, decided to name her Autumn, since she was born in the month of November.

When I married my husband Bill, I was thrilled to be marrying into this, big, close knit family. And I was immediately touched by the fact that Terry and Russell were not only committed to one another, but they were also committed to raising their children in a loving, godly home. I felt blessed to have them as my sister and brother-in-law. Terry is Bill's only sister and we love her very much

Soon the bouncing baby girl of the family became a toddler, and she was loved by everyone. This little angel never met a stranger, (no way!) and she seemed to love every person with whom she came in contact.

Autumn had two older brothers, Justin and Cole, who were determined to protect her and keep her out of trouble. As this adorable child grew into a very beautiful young teenager, her brothers, who loved her very much, became even more protective toward her.

In her early teens she began entering beauty pageants in Saluda, and different cities around the state of South Carolina. It didn't surprise anyone when she entered and won many of the local and state competitions.

Although Autumn started winning beauty pageants on a regular basis, and becoming more and more popular, it never seemed to go to her head. She always remained a sweet, loving young woman, and in return, it seemed as if the entire community loved her back.

One Friday night in early November 2006, Bill and I had just turned the light out and were almost asleep, when I thought I heard the phone ringing. When I finally realized the phone was actually ringing, half asleep, I jumped up and ran to look for it. I finally found one in the den, but just as I picked up the receiver, it quit ringing.

I returned to bed thinking - it must have been someone who dialed a wrong number. Five or ten minutes later, when I was almost back to sleep the phone rang again, and once more, I jumped up and ran to the den to get it, but as soon as I said hello, they hung up. Since the phone that was usually on the nightstand beside the bed, had apparently been left in another room, I took the den phone to bed, and told my husband, Bill, "If it rings again, this time you answer it and maybe they won't hang up."

Sure enough in about five minutes, I heard it ring. Bill picked it up and said, "Hello!"

Next I heard him say, "Oh no," When he said, "Oh no," again, I was afraid something bad had happened.

After a while he started to cry and say, "You've got to be kidding. I'll get up and leave now and get there as quickly as I can!"

When Bill hung up the phone I asked, "What in the world happened?"

I was expecting him to say one of his brothers had passed away, since just six months before, the oldest brother had died of a heart attack.

Instead to my horror, I heard him say, "Autumn's dead!"

I said, "What?"

Once again, he said, "Autumn's dead!"

I asked Bill, "What happened to her, she can't be dead?"

He said, "She died in a car wreck on the way home from spending the evening with her boyfriend's family. She must have swerved to miss a deer and she hit a tree about seventy-five yards from the house. The vehicle caught on fire and she burned to death.

What's horrible is that her boyfriend, Joey, left his house to look for her, when she didn't call to let him know she made it home safely. He saw the fire trucks and EMS going out toward the house, so he called Terry and Russell to see if Autumn was at home.

They told him, 'No, she hasn't gotten home yet.'"

We later found out, that at this point, Joey started screaming, "No Autumn, No, Oh, God no!", then his cell phone went dead. Terry looked out the window and saw blue lights flashing from the top of a patrol car. She screamed to the rest of the family, "Autumn's been in a wreck, hurry, go help her, please!"

Autumn's daddy, Russell and her brother Justin flew out the door, while her brother Cole stayed in the house with Terry, her Mama.

Cole said, "Mama, let's pray!"

And pray they did, asking God, "Please, don't take Autumn, please, we love her, Lord, please, let her be okay!"

Finally Cole said, "Mama, will you be alright, I've got to go there?"

Terry told him to go, and she continued praying until she heard a howling cry coming from her son Justin as he came up the steps and he tells his Mama, "Autumn's gone, she's dead."

Justin wraps his arms around Terry, who's crying and in shock, at what has just taken place, and all that has ,so suddenly, happened to her and to her family, that would change their lives forever.

Bill said, "I'll throw my clothes on and go and I'll call you as soon as I get there. You and Michael and Denise can drive over tomorrow."

Michael and Denise are our grandson and his wife, and it was such a blessing that they were living with us right then, so they were able to drive with me over to Saluda to the funeral.

I couldn't believe what I had just heard and what apparently had just taken place; our beautiful little niece was dead. How and why would God let this happen? Soon, I would find out the answer to that question.

Bill was weeping, when he called later that day and said, "Sugar, this is the most horrible thing I've ever seen or been through. It is so terrible seeing Terry and Russell going through this. And even Justin and Cole are completely torn up.

Terry hasn't stopped crying and asking everyone, "Can someone, please, tell me she was dead before the fire started? Can someone, please, tell me?"

I think they'll be having visitation tomorrow night and the church and graveside services on Monday afternoon. So you, Michael and Denise can wait and come Monday morning and still get here in time for the services."

Every time Bill called he would be crying and sobbing, for he loved Autumn, as if she were one of our own grandchildren. His heart, as well as mine, was breaking for the family left behind to deal with this terrible tragedy.

Bill called back the next day from the visitation at the funeral home. He said, "This is unbelievable, there have been almost one thousand people that have been here, (Little did he know that, before the visitation was over, by midnight that night, two thousand five hundred people would file through the funeral home, and sign the condolence book.) and that's out of a town of twenty-two thousand people.

That Monday, Michael, Denise and I drove over to Saluda for the funeral. On the drive over I had been thinking about the situation and it seemed, as if the Lord expressed to me out loud, that Jesus, was walking down that road waiting for Autumn, and as she passed by He simply snatched her out of the car and away they went to heaven. The car crashed, because for all intents and purposes, it was driverless. I decided that as soon as I got to Terry and Russell's house I had to tell Terry what the Lord had revealed to me.

When we arrived at the house, it was packed with people and yet Terry came running to greet us. I took the family a poem that I had written for Autumn and gave it to her. I also told her what the Lord laid on my heart during our drive over.

Terry immediately, upon reading the poem said she wanted the preacher to read it at the service. She asked me if that would be okay and of course, I told her that would be fine.

We left the house in our car, following the funeral coach, and as we got closer to town we noticed policemen at each corner directing traffic. Then as we got about a block from the church the entire area turned into a parking lot, but the immediate family members following the funeral coach were able to park beside the church in reserved spaces.

When we entered the church we saw that it was completely packed, and people were standing all the way around the walls with the balcony full as well. The crowd outside extended all the way around the building and about ten or fifteen rows deep. (I later found out for visitation, the line was so long some people waited in lines three to four blocks long, and for some it took several hours to get into the funeral home).

Once we got into the church and the service started, there wasn't a single dry eye in the place. Men, women, children, black, white, red or brown, all shapes and sizes and people of all ages, were there crying together. I've never seen anything like it and I've been in the cemetery and funeral home business for twenty- three years.

An amazing thing happened, when the pastor said, "I really feel that Jesus was standing on that highway, just waiting for Autumn to pass by so He could reach in and take her right out of that car. She wasn't even in the car when it hit that tree." I was sitting there hoping Terry picked up on the fact, that the Lord had reiterated what I had told her back at the house.

The testimonies were abundant and the service lasted over three hours. Everyone wanting to tell the people about how Autumn had touched and changed their lives. One young black teenage boy stood up and said, "Autumn was my only friend, she was the only person black or white that acted like I mattered. She would take me over to her house to bake cookies, and one time had me on the couch with my head in her lap, plucking my eyebrows. She was my best and only friend and always will be." I thought this young man was going to pass out he was crying so hard when people passed by the closed casket. He kept repeating, "This can't be for real, it can't be! She was my best friend!"

Another young man said, "I had just moved here and the kids at the school would shun me and act like I didn't exist. Autumn saw me sitting on the floor, in the corner of the cafeteria, eating my lunch by myself.

When she got up and told the girls she was sitting with what she was going to do, they said, "What do you want to do that for?"

She came to me and said, "What are you doing sitting on the floor?" Come on get up from there and come sit at my table from now on." When she told the other girls why she did it, they looked like they felt ashamed.

Next the mother of the young man she'd been dating, got up and said, "Autumn changed our whole family, and we couldn't wait for her to someday be our daughter-in-law, only we felt more like she was a daughter."
The son was hysterically weeping, when he stood up and said, "Autumn wouldn't go out with me for two years, she would only be my friend, until finally she got me to go to church. Due to her influence I gave my life to the Lord and I've had a whole new life. I'll never be able to replace her. My mother was right about Autumn changing our family, for my Dad" he paused and glanced over at his dad in the crowd, "never hugged or kissed me and never told me he loved me, until she came into our lives and her love changed us all. Autumn loved everyone unconditionally."

Senior citizens came in wheelchairs, and told about how Autumn would go to the nursing home where they lived and tuck them in bed, kiss them goodnight and tell them she loved them. They were all heartbroken and sad that she would never be coming back.

I could go on and on telling about the testimonies that I heard at that funeral. The pastor said that Autumn probably touched the lives of people in nearly every family in Saluda.

Well, after the funeral, anyone who had been there could understand why the Lord in His wisdom took her home. The lives that were touched and changed not only by her life, but by her death as well are too numerous to have imagined. And everyone thought (and rightfully so) that Autumn was the happiest person and the most outgoing person they had ever seen. But what could be greater than the greatest things on earth. Why, the great things waiting for God's children in heaven, of course! Autumn already experienced the best the world had to offer and there was no place to go but to heaven to be with Jesus.

Autumn got promoted to a higher plane, and when she arrived at her new destination she got to hear the Lord say," Autumn, well done, thou good and faithful servant! Welcome home!"

Friends, Autumn, left an unbelievable legacy and testimony for her loved ones and friends to remember. What kind of legacy will you leave behind when you depart from this world and where are you headed when it comes time foro you to go?

Don't wait too late to make up your mind, for you may not have tomorrow! Autumn had no idea, nor did her family that she was leaving this world that day, but was ready to go whenever the time came. Are you ready? It's always better to be safe than sorry.

God Bless You!

Autumn's in Heaven

Autumn is a special season,
Leaves turning, red and gold...
It's that wonderful time of year...
Just before the winter's cold.

It's a time of awesome beauty
Other seasons can't compare.
But when old winter's blast arrives,
Trees and shrubs start looking bare.

Once there was another Autumn...
So loved by one and all...
Special to Jesus her Savior...
On whose name she'd often call.

The hosts of heaven loved her so,
And they watched from above...
...As she showered all those around...
...With her special kind of love.

When Jesus called her home to...
That land beyond the sky,
Many tears were shed for they found...
No time to say goodbye.

We must all remember that our...
...Children aren't ours alone,
They belong to God in heaven
And to us they're just on loan.

Our loving Lord is free to call
Us home at any time,
It might be me or you or it could
Be a child of yours or mine

Angels shouted, "Hallelujah", as Autumn
Stepped up on heaven's shore,
Seeing all the glory...she thought,
"Golly, who could ask for more?

So loved ones rejoice don't mourn,
Autumn's happy as can be.
Living with Jesus in a mansion now
For all of Eternity.

She's having a blast with friends and...
All the loved ones waiting there,
If we could ask, "Won't you come back?"
She'd say, "No way, I wouldn't dare!

But I'll be here to greet you when
You arrive in Beulah Land,
And we'll see the sights in heaven
Just walking hand in hand.

Words could never describe this place
And all that God has in store,
Why, if people knew the truth - they'd
Be rushing right to the door.

When at last you're up in heaven...
Then you'll be able to see,
And I can't wait to hear you saying...
"Gee! God had all this for me?"

Don't Let Me Out of Your Arms

Have you ever wished that the Lord had made us robots, so that we would all automatically obey Him? Seems to be a reasonable thought doesn't it, after all we're so much happier when we're obedient to His will and to His Word. It should make it easier to glorify Him by our actions, don't you think so?

In my own life, at times, when I've messed up in some way, I have said, "Lord, can't I just give you my permission to make me Your robot? After all - it's with my free will to make choices, that I'm choosing to let You do it, I want you to, won't You, please?"

I want to be an obedient child and I am only happy when I am. And yet the only time I obey is when I'm emptied out of myself and letting the Lord fill me with Himself. And then allowing Him to minister and do His will through me.(Then we can't take any credit for anything for He does it all, we simply surrender) But it is only pleasing to our Father, when we choose, by our own free will, to let Him fill us up and work through us; to carry us and all of our burdens and baggage.

I don't think there's anything wrong in saying, "Lord, when I try to get out of Your arms, just hold me tighter still!" Since with those words, I'm asking Him to let the Holy Spirit convict me before I fall into any sin of rebellion, before it starts taking hold, for I know how miserable it can be wandering around on my own.

Have you ever had one of your own children wander off in the store when they were small, and they were crying their little eyes out. You might have been right on the next isle (very close) but out of sight. Something enticed them to walk away and soon they looked up and realized you weren't there. They immediately start to panic and yet once you come into view they are so happy and so are you.

It's the same way with us in our relationship with the Lord. One minute everything is great and the next thing you know something is trying to get our attention. Sometimes we resist, but there are those times we give in; then suddenly we find ourselves getting all out of sorts, and we'll stay that way until we get back where we belong, safe in our Father's arms.

Rebellion can be very costly to us spiritually, physically, mentally, emotionally or even financially, so let's ask our Father not to let us out of His strong, loving arms; even if we should wiggle to get down, just like our children have at times. Let's just say, "Father, hold me tighter still!"

Read Psalms chapter 51 and focus on verse 12: Grant me a willing spirit to sustain me.

Read Psalms chapter 143 and focus on verse10: Teach me to do Your will, for You are my God. May Your good Spirit lead me on level ground.

Don't Let Me Out of Your Arms

Lord, where are you - I've lost my way,
Please, show me that You care.
I pray and fear You haven't heard,
I need to know You're there.

I feel that You're so far away,
And prayers go unheard,
I pray and then it seems, as if
You haven't heard a word.

My prayer requests are mounting
Higher every day.
I feel so lost and lonely now,
I don't know what to say.

It seems You've turned Your face away,
I don't know what's gone wrong.
I thought I heard the Spirit say,
"Come home where you belong."

Lord, You mean it was really me
I turned my back on You?
I can't believe I'd do that but
I guess it's really true.

I love You Lord, how could I let...
The world just crowd You out?
I lost my focus and too soon
Forgot what You're about.

So, thank You for reminding me...
That You're the only way,
And from now on, please, call my name,
If I should start to stray...

...For when I think about it all...
Without You life's a bore,
I hope that from now on I won't
Be roaming anymore.

You're my joy and happiness and
In darkness You're my light,
You're the One who wins my battle
When I'm too weak to fight...

You give me the strength to make it
When I want to give up,
And when I feel so empty Lord,
You always fill my cup.

There's nothing in this whole wide world
That I could ever find,
That blesses me like You do in...
My heart, my soul and mind.

So whenever I am tempted
Just hold me close to you,
Don't let me get out of Your arms...
No matter what I do.

And if I should wiggle and squirm
Just hold me tighter still.
For happiness will only come
From being in Your will.

Thank You Father for listening
To this little prayer.
I guess at times I need reminding
Of just how much You care.

It's Easy?

Friend, have you ever been just a little bit envious of someone? Perhaps it was at a time when you found yourself going through some pretty heavy trials, physically or financially. Regardless of the circumstances you couldn't help but wonder why your unsaved neighbor seemed to have it made in every area of life. They were: prospering tremendously in their profession, their marriage seemed to be so happy and solid, they apparently never have any problems with their children, their whole family always looks like they're in good health and they have that huge, gorgeous home and that brand new Hummer(of course you wouldn't want one but it sure would be nice to have something newer and bigger), and golly, they sure have lots of friends.

Do you find yourself suddenly falling into a critical mode? Starting sentences about the neighbors with, "I'll bet the reason they...", when you talk to your spouse or others about them?

Friend, first of all, envy is a sin, second concern yourself with their soul. Have you shared Christ with that family? If not, why not? Gossip is a sin as well, and often you cause others to join you in your sin. Even if the family is doing some things wrong the problem on your part is that you need to worry about the log in your eye instead of the splinter in someone else's.

It's very possible that some of your own trials and tribulations will improve when you get your priorities in order. Sin and especially unconfessed sin in our lives can cause hardships, trials and stress to hold us in a very strong grip. We must recognize our own areas of weakness and anything that might have a hold on us that we need to throw off and from which we need to break free and take the proper steps to get our lives back right with the Lord. Start by confessing all known sin in our lives.

Gossip and criticism are usually a sign of being out of fellowship for when a believer is out of fellowship they live and act like an unbeliever, they need to immediately turn back to the Lord for the longer they wait the easier it becomes to put it off and to put our spiritual life on the back burner.

Saint of God, don't be envious for if that other person never puts their faith in Christ they are receiving their reward now and it's only temporary, yours comes later and it's eternal.

David in Psalms 73 shows us a perfect example of our humanity. He didn't understand what was going on until He entered the sanctuary of God.(Got back in fellowship)

Read Psalms chapter 101 and focus on verse 5: Whoever slanders his neighbor, him will I put to silence.

Read Psalms chapter 73 and focus on verses 2-5: But as for me, my feet had almost slipped, I had nearly lost my foothold. For I envied the arrogant when I saw the prosperity of the wicked. They have no struggles; their bodies are healthy and strong. They are free from the burdens common to man, they are not plagued by human ills.

Verses 13-17: Surely in vain have I kept my heart pure; in vain have I washed my hands in innocence. All day long I have been plagued; I have been punished every morning. If I had said, "I will speak thus," I would have betrayed your children. When I tried to understand all this, it was oppressive to me, till I entered the sanctuary of God; then I understood their final destiny.

It's Easy?

Why is it, Lord, sometimes it seems
It's easy living life?
Yet there are days it feels as if
It's always constant strife.

I see those who have no problems,
It seems that all goes well,
But by the way they live their lives
It makes it hard to tell.

I must admit there are those times
When envious I've been,
Yet when I read Your Word it says
That envy is a sin.

When I see others with no woes
I can't help but question,
How to have the easy life and
What is Your suggestion?

Well, quickly You remind me
They're getting their reward.
And I'll get mine in heaven but
The wait is just so hard!

You let me know that I have read
The answer in Your Word,
Yet sometimes by the way I act
It seems I haven't heard.

Jesus, warned that in this life,
We'll have tribulations,
But He has overcome this world
With all of its frustrations.

So now I find that living life
Is easy when we know,
To give Him all our problems
While living here below.

And then each day we'll find ourselves -
Having a lot more fun...
If we bundle up our troubles -
And give them to God's Son

Direct-Line/No Waiting

Friend, when you become a child of the King it comes with so many wonderful blessings. You are not only born into a wonderful, loving, extended family with great brothers and sisters, but you are adopted by the number one Dad in the universe.

Your Father always has an open door and a listening ear, and he's always ready and waiting to hear from you. And any time the weather turns threatening you're always free to take your spot under His wing, until things calm down and the dark clouds pass on by.

You'll find your Father God, is always dependable and when you pick up the phone and give Him a call, you'll always get through, the line is never busy and you won't be put on hold. Every time we call, He answers so readily, and you never have to worry about whether or not you've interrupted something, and He'll always be totally interested in what you have to say.

You will have the peace of knowing that all things do work together for good in your life, and in the lives of all your brothers and sisters in your adopted family.

You become an heir of the King of Kings and the Lord of Lords and you'll be able to look forward to spending all of Eternity in heaven with the whole entire family.

The list of blessings could go on, so don't put it off, come and join our wonderful family today. You won't ever be sorry!

Read Galatians chapter 4 and then focus on verse 7: So you are no longer a slave, but a son; and since you are a son, God has made you also an heir.

Direct-Line/No Waiting

Being the child of a King has
Some great benefits,
Many meant for times when you're
About to lose your wits.

God has awesome special blessings
For all who seek to do His will;
When you're feeling sad and lonely,
His love just fits the bill.

The King will safely keep you...
Right in the palm of His hand,
And all of His strongest angel's are
Available on demand.

Each one of the Lord's children has
Their own direct line,
They'll find He's never too busy
He'll answer every time.

You'll never be told you must call back or
Be endlessly put on hold,
God is always ready to answer and
He talks with young and old.

His children never have to wait,
He listens to them all,
But you'll need His number if you
Want to give Him a call.

When you accept the Lord - you'll have
Your own private line,
So you'll be able to call no matter
What the place or time.

You'll have unlimited calling
Why wait another day,
God is waiting to hear from you -
So, call Him right away.

I Thought

Friend, have you ever truly believed, and even said to yourself, "If only...",(you can fill in the blank). It might say - if only we didn't have so many bills or if only we had a bigger house, a nicer car, or more and better friends. It might even say, if only I could lose weight or if only my husband or wife gave me more attention. Of course we could go on forever, since there are so many "if onlys."

Sadly, many people honestly believe that if their circumstances were different, life would automatically be better, but they are terribly mistaken."If only" we understood that happiness is fleeting and nothing this world has to offer can bring lasting happiness apart from the Lord. There are people who have everything this world has to offer and yet they are still miserable, some to the point of attempting suicide and others are even successful at their attempt.

Every person ever born has a special spot with the Lord, one where the Lord had a wonderful, fulfilling life planned for them. Due to their free will and the bad choices they make, most people never find that spot, and although they know the Lord they miss out on the joy that was theirs. They'll be in heaven but they miss out on so much during their lifetime on earth. Then there are those who never find the Lord at all, and they not only miss their spot, but they miss heaven as well.

But for those who find that spot the Lord had for them, they will have happiness and joy throughout life. They'll have it during the good times and the bad, happy times and sad, for the happiness is found in, and comes with, the spot. The spot itself is found in the center of God's will and the devil will do all he can to keep you from finding it, and when you do find it, he'll try to draw you out of the spot.   Don't let him!

Joy is found in the spot right in the center of God's will and that is where you are when you are walking in the Spirit.

Read Galatians chapter 5 and then focus on verse 22: But the fruit of the Spirit is love, JOY, peace, gentleness, goodness, faith, meekness and self-control. Read Isaiah chapter 35 and then focus on verses 9-10: But only the redeemed will walk there, and the ransomed of the Lord will return. They will enter Zion with singing; everlasting joy will crown their heads. Gladness and joy will overtake them, and sorrow and sighing will flee away.

I Thought

I thought I knew what I wanted...
Fame and riches untold,
But joy never comes by seeking
Worldly pleasures, silver or gold.

I thought I'd find all that I sought...
In cars, houses and land;
But soon found out earthly treasures...
Would easily slip from my hand.

I then began to realize,
All of my thoughts were wrong;
Real joy can only be found in...
That special place where I belong.

For each of God's children has their
Very own private spot,
Found in the center of His will,
Whether they choose that spot or not.

Now, in that place His children find,
True joy and peace within...
And those who stay and abide there,
Can lay down their burden of sin.

I thought I knew what I wanted...
Then Jesus called my name,
And from that moment on I knew...
...That life...would never be the same.

You may think you know what you want,
But choose to take your place;
Set aside for you long ago
By God's wonderful love and grace.

The choice is up to you, my friend,
But in the end you'll find...
That choice will either set you free,
Or it will leave you in a bind.

Yes, free to have all the blessings
God has in store for you,
Or to be bound by wrong decisions...
...Believing Satan's lies are true.

The Angelic Conflict

Many people worship angels and others doubt they exist. In the Word of God it mentions angels many times, solidly reinforcing the fact that they are real. Another thing that testifies to their existence is personal experience. Have you ever had a close call and you could almost feel the brush of their wings as they undertook to protect you? I've had some near misses in traffic, I've almost taken a serious fall and numerous other episodes of angelic intervention have taken place on my behalf, and on that of several other family members

Although we are not to worship angels, as I wrote in the poem "My Guardian Angel" (in my first book), I know I've been a tough assignment and a fulltime job, so, when I get home to heaven - although I don't believe we'll need their protection in heaven - I want to find my own guardian angel and thank him for all his hard work and for all the overtime he had to put in because of me.

There are good angels, the angels of the Lord and the bad angels that do Satan's bidding. These awesome beings are in a constant battle in the unseen spiritual realm. And just as I have felt my angel working in my behalf, so I have felt Satan's angels trying to interfere in things the Lord had called me to do. In fact, the interference I've experienced just trying to get this second book to the publisher has been overwhelming. My computer crashing and me losing all my work and now still having constant unexplained problems with it. That old devil simply doesn't want us serving the Lord in any capacity.

But let's all make a commitment to stand our ground and not give him a single inch, just simply pay no attention to him for he's already been defeated.

Read Hebrews chapter 13 and then focus on verses 1-2: Keep on loving

one another as brothers. Do not forget to entertain strangers, for by so doing some people have entertained angels, without knowing it.

Read Psalms chapter 91 and then focus on verses 11-12 For he will command His angels concerning you, to keep you in all your ways, and they will lift you up in their hands, so that you will not strike your foot against a stone.

The Angelic Conflict

God's angels fight a battle in
The darkest realms unknown,
Protecting His dear children from
The evil being sown.

These warriors are in the battle
To guard the souls of men.
While Satan's angels do their best,
Trying each fight to win.

It seems the war goes on and on,
Angels using sword and shield...
Each one fighting for the people
To bow before their God and yield.

Satan's forces fighting hard
To crush the Angels of Light.
Christ the Mighty Warrior leads
God's Army day and night.

The battle goes on raging for
What seems like forever.
But will old Satan's angels win?
Absolutely never!

Christ Himself won the victory,
Many long years ago.
Yet some still ask the question, "Just,
How do you know that's so?"

I know for I found the answer,
In God's Holy Word.
Still, some read the Bible and act,
As if they'd never heard.

God's angels will keep on fighting
Although this war is won;
They could never lose the battle for...
Their leader is God's Son

The end has been decided, so
No need to doubt or fear.
Soon Christ will come to take us home,
And we'll be leaving here.

The Gift

Dear One, Have you ever thought about the fact that as children of God, we receive so many wonderful blessings; and yet, what did our Savior receive while He was on this earth? I know simply the thought of the gifts that He bought us with His death on the cross, should it not motivate us all the more to give our lives to Him, as a gift to lay at His feet.

The truth is that there is no way we could ever out give or out love the Lord. For if we give Him our lives He in turn gives us so many blessings, that they cannot be counted. The first gifts are our salvation and heaven for eternity; then the list just goes on and on from there. He gave up his throne in glory, came to earth and was mocked, beaten and abused, then suffered and died on the cross in our place; all because of His immeasurable love.

We don't have to give Him anything back for our gifts, for they have no strings attached, they are absolutely free. And yet shouldn't it make us want to surrender everything to the Lord? Not only because we love Him, but we know when we do that we will be so tremendously blessed. It almost seems selfish to surrender all to Jesus knowing ahead of time, what we'll receive in return. Jesus only gives and we only receive.

Just think, Dear One, we gave Jesus, a whip, a crown, some nails and a cross and He gave us everything we need for life and godliness, as well as unlimited, unconditional love. It's just awesome. God the Father gave us the gift of His Son. His Son gave us the gift of life eternal.

Read John chapter 4 and then focus on verse 10: Jesus answered her, "If you knew the gift of God and who it is that asks you for a drink, you would have asked Him and He would have given you living water.

Read John chapter 19 and then focus on verse 2: And the soldiers twisted together a crown of thorns and put it on His head.

The Gift

A whip, a crown, some nails, a cross,
Nothing of any real worth,
But things that were meant for our Savior,
Right from the day of His birth.

On the day that He was born,
The angels began to sing,
Soon the Magi would bring Him gifts,
Only fit for a king.

But the world was not ready
To accept this precious One,
They criticized and abused Him,
Although He was God's Son...

The One God sent to save mankind
Gave up His glorious throne;
Became a living sacrifice,
Suffered and died alone.

The greatest gift ever given
Soon rejected by men,
Who sadly chose to continue,
Living their life in sin.

The gift that God freely gave us,
All because of His love,
He sent to this ungodly world
Straight from heaven above.

My Friend, please, accept your free gift.
For God paid a high price,
In fact, the gift was so costly,
Jesus paid with His life.

Can you imagine such love?
A King dies on a tree,
For lost, unworthy sinners,
Just like you and me.

And what does the Savior ask us,
To do on our part?
To simply invite Him to come in...
And make His home in our heart.

Then as soon as He moves in
We'll find joy so sublime,
That only comes from knowing Jesus,
And being His for all time.

Martyr for a Minute

Why is it my friend, that so many people don't mind doing things for others when it's convenient and it won't put them out? And then they act as if what they did was some big deal.

If you only had some beans to eat and you saw someone on the street with no beans, would you share your beans, even if you only had enough to last one day?

Would you be willing to lay down your life for one of your family members, how about a friend, even for an enemy? Or where would you draw the line?

There are those who do what they want to do for people and then they want to make sure the world knows what they did. They actually do what they do, not for the one who's in need, but because they want to make themselves look good in front of others.

We are supposed to live a life that's yielded to the Lord, so we are to let Him do whatever He wants to for others, through us. And it's no big deal for it's not us doing it - it's our Father God, doing it through us. We can't take any credit.

Read Romans chapter 12 and then focus on verses 1-2: Therefore, I beseech you brethren, that you present your bodies as a living sacrifice, holy and acceptable unto God, which is your reasonable service(It's no big deal) and be not conformed to this world, but be ye transformed by the renewing of your mind, that you may prove what is that good and perfect and acceptable will of God.

Read Philippians chapter 2 and then focus on verses 3-4: Do nothing out of selfish ambition or vain conceit, but in humility consider others better than yourselves. Each of you should look not only to your own interests, but also to the interests of others.

Martyr for a Minute

Do you sacrifice when giving
Your money or your time,
And what would be your attitude
If it was your last dime?

What if you only had enough
To last a single day,
If someone came along with less
I wonder what you'd say.

When you take time to go to church
You think it's some big deal,
But don't you think that you should go
Because your faith is real?

If God gives you the chance to help
Someone along the way,
Then don't you waste time asking just
How much you'll have to pay.

If you were asked to give your life
To save that of a friend,
Could you say yes...or is that where
Your giving then would end?

Could you choose to give your all for
Anyone else's good,
Or would you walk away instead
Of doing as you should?

Martyr for a minute is what
Most people seem to be,
Doing what they want - when they want
Hoping the world will see.

But when the Devil calls your name
Don't pay him any heed;
Surrender your all to Jesus
And let Him take the lead.

...For Satan hates to see a saint
Doing the will of God,
He does his best to stop them as...
They walk this earthly sod.

But let the Lord use you as His
Instrument of blessing;
And Satan will give up when he
Sees he's not progressing.

The Lonely Boy

How many lonely people are out there, passing us by on the street and in the stores? How many are in their homes, and cars pass by the house not knowing that there is someone inside who's very lonely and sad. It breaks your heart, all the lonely people, but it's truly sad as well, that most people don't really care.

There are those who could watch their neighbor being put out in the street and they wouldn't even offer to take them in until they could get on their feet. It might get a little dirt on their carpet or be too much of a bother in general. If only they knew what they're missing. It is such a blessing and a privilege to let the Lord help others through you; and when you do He'll bless you immensely. And you never know the impact it might make for years to come.

You just might be taking in one of God's angels, just like it says in Hebrews chapter 13 and verses 1-2: And be not forgetful to entertain strangers for thereby, some have entertained angels unaware.

Read Matthew chapter 25 and then focus on verses 33-46:

When the Son of Man comes in his glory, and all the angels with him, he will sit on his throne in heavenly glory. All the nations will be gathered before him, and he will separate the people one from another as a shepherd separates the sheep from the goats. He will put the sheep on his right and the goats on his left.

Then the King will say to those on his right, 'Come, you who are blessed by my Father; take your inheritance, the kingdom prepared for you since the creation of the world. For I was hungry and you gave me something to eat, I was thirsty and you gave me something to drink, I was a stranger and you invited me in, I needed clothes and you clothed me, I was sick and you looked after me, I was in prison and you came to visit me.'

"Then the righteous will answer him, 'Lord, when did we see you hungry and feed you, or thirsty and give you something to drink? When did we see you a stranger and invite you in, or needing clothes and clothe you? When did we see you sick or in prison and go to visit you?'

"The King will reply, 'I tell you the truth, whatever you did for one of the least of these brothers of mine, you did for me.'

"Then he will say to those on his left, 'Depart from me, you who are cursed, into the eternal fire prepared for the devil and his angels. For I was hungry and you gave me nothing to eat, I was thirsty and you gave me nothing to drink, I was a stranger and you did not invite me in, I needed clothes and you did not clothe me, I was sick and in prison and you did not look after me.'

"They also will answer, 'Lord, when did we see you hungry or thirsty or a stranger or needing clothes or sick or in prison, and did not help you?'

"He will reply, 'I tell you the truth, whatever you did not do for one of the least of these, you did not do for me.'

"Then they will go away to eternal punishment, but the righteous to eternal life."

The Lonely Boy

The young man stands at the window,
He's looking so forlorn.
It could almost break your heart,
That look is not the norm.

You wonder what's the matter and
Wish you could ring the bell;
Instead you drive on by and he
Withdraws into his shell.

He hoped when you slowed down, that you'd
Be coming to the door:
Since his folks passed away, there are
No visits anymore.

He doesn't go to school, they might
Find out that he's alone;
Instead he lives in darkness always
Listening for the phone.

No one ever calls for they don't
Know that anyone's there.
But even if they knew it then
They probably wouldn't care.

There's not a soul, to tell this lonely
Boy about a friend:
Who loves him very much and He
Will love him till the end.

A creaky old car pulls right up
Just in front of his door;
Out steps this dear little lady - who's,
A Christian to the core.

Sitting at home she felt the urge,
To find some doors to knock;
When she got to the young man's door,
He barely turned the lock.

He didn't know who it was...and feared
She would take him away.
At last he slightly opened the door,
But didn't know what to say.

The lady told him of the One
Who removes all doubts and fears.
And lovingly said, "If you'll trust -
Jesus will dry your tears."

God knew just what this young man lacked
A friendship with the King;
If he put his faith in the Lord - soon
He wouldn't need a thing.

So he decided to believe,
And was given life anew.
Friend, if you don't possess it - you
Can have that new life too

This story has a happy ending
He'd never again have to roam,
The old lady loved him so much,
She took him to live in her home.

Would There Be Enough Evidence?

Believer, with all the turmoil going on in this world, what's next? Who knows? The devil is doing his best to turn people, if not nations against Christians. If we try to stand up for what's right, then we are labeled trouble-makers. I personally think that as the days and times draw to a close, it will get worse and worse.

If it ever got to the point that we were arrested for being a Christian, and taking a stand, would there be enough evidence to convict us? Friend, I truly hope so, for if not we've been living as under-cover Christians.

Can people see Jesus in all that we do? Can they see us living by the Word of God, letting Christ live in and work through us? We should be found guilty in the first degree, thrown under the jail and even then the prison guards should see us living the Word right there in the midst of the other inmates. That's the way Jesus and the disciples and early Christians lived and they dragged them out into the streets and stoned them to death, fed them to lions, burned them at the stake and tore them in pieces. They stood their ground and lived what they believed. Would we?

Read Hebrews chapter 11 and please read the entire chapter and then focus on verses 32-38:

And what more shall I say? I do not have time to tell about Gideon, Barak, Samson, Jephthah, David, Samuel and the prophets, who through faith conquered kingdoms, administered justice, and gained what was promised; who shut the mouths of lions, quenched the fury of the flames, and escaped the edge of the sword; whose weakness was turned to strength; and who became powerful in battle and routed foreign armies. Women received back their dead, raised to life again. Others were tortured and refused to be released, so that they might gain a better resurrection. Some faced jeers and flogging, while still others were chained and put in prison. They were stoned; they were sawed in two; they were put to death by the sword. They went about in sheepskins and goatskins, destitute, persecuted and mistreated:

"the world was not worthy of them. They wandered in deserts and mountains, and in caves and holes in the ground."

Would There Be Enough Evidence?

In this life that we live, who knows
What each new day may hold...
Will the sky be clear or cloudy or
Will it be warm or cold?

Will the day be filled with peace and calm
In this our earthly realm?
Will we let Christ steer our ship or...
Will we be at the helm?

If suddenly we found ourselves
In a deadly battle...
With people of faith being rounded up,
Then put in pens like cattle.

As we were put on trial before...
...A jury of our peers,
Would we stand up and testify
Or...be overwhelmed by fears?

If we were tried in court, and being
A Christian was our crime,
Would there be so much evidence
That we'd be doing time?

For if we were truly believers
Both judge and jury should know,
Unless for a lack of evidence
They'd have to let us go

Hopefully being Christians we would
Be guilty of many infractions,
And others should be able to tell
Not by words but by our actions

Would our captors know by our deeds
Prison's where we should be;
And once we're there to stay, then they
Can throw away the key.

But if they had no witnesses
They'd have to set us free,
Showing there'd been many good works
Never done by you or me.

Noah's Ark

Dear One, what would we have done if we had been in Noah's shoes? Can you imagine being told to build this huge boat by Almighty God? You're told it's going to rain when it had never rained before, and for the next one hundred and ten years you have a bunch of nosey people laughing and making fun of you. You must remember, they had never seen rain and I doubt if any of them had ever talked with or heard personally from God, so it's understandable that they would act that way.

I wonder if Noah had days that he wanted to say, "Forget this! This is too hard and besides, Lord, I can't take listening to these foolish mockers any longer." Think about how a person can get on your nerves, but at least you can usually get away from them.

Sadly, Noah warned these disobedient people the whole time he was building on the ark. Isn't that just like the people today, you can warn them that the Lord's coming soon and they just scoff at you. You can tell the unbelievers that they can't afford to put off accepting Christ, for they may not have tomorrow and usually they say something like, "Maybe one of these days, but I'm just not ready now."

The same way the people in Noah's day probably ran to the ark when it started to rain, but it was too late, the door was locked; the people in hell like the rich young ruler, wanted Lazarus to send some one back to warn his family, and Lazarus said he couldn't but they wouldn't listen any way.

Never quit trying to win souls to the Lord, for until they take their last breath, it's not too late. Be faithful in your calling, just like Noah. Noah and his family were saved due to his faithfulness. Even though everyone else may be unfaithful, you must remain faithful.

Read chapters 6-7 in Genesis and focus on 7:1 The Lord, then said to Noah, "Go into the ark, you and your whole family, because I have found you righteous in this generation."

Noah's Ark

Noah lived in the Bible days
And obeyed God in all his ways,
The Lord said it would start to rain
Yet, he never did complain.

Things on earth had gotten so bad
That God was now very mad,
He told Noah to build a boat
Soon he'd need it to stay afloat.

Then the Lord said, "Because of sin
I'll just do away with men.
I'll send down a terrible flood
Then start all over with new blood.

Noah never saw rain before
but...
Soon there'd be more and more.
All the animals would come to him
For none of them would be able to swim.

This would be a horrible sight
People trying to swim all night.
As Noah built - people made fun
Not knowing soon they'd start to run.

God told Noah, "Get the animals in
Very soon rain will begin.
You and your family must get on board
With my entire animal hoard.

The rain came down for forty days
And all aboard obeyed God's ways.
They all knew to make it through
Each must do what He told them to.

The rain stopped and the Ark set down
Noah's family looked around
The animals came out two by two
Each one knew just what to do.

God said, "Go replenish the earth,
You've just gone through a brand new birth
I'm starting over with life anew,
And Noah, it's all going to start with you."

You Ask Me Why

Friend, have you ever wanted someone you loved to accept Christ as their Savior and you were willing to do anything to see that happen. Personally, I hounded my parents and my brother and his wife to come to church. My parents, after they came and got saved and then baptized in the river, later told me, that they had decided to come one time just to shut me up; and then they said they were going to tell me it just wasn't for them. Surprise! The first Sunday they came they both found the Lord. Later a similar event took place in my brother and sister-in-law's lives as well.

I have always felt that if I had the cure for cancer and knew it for certain, and I had a friend or loved one that had cancer, but they ran from me, because they were afraid of shots and the cure came only in the form of a shot; I wouldn't hesitate to hit them on the head, knock them out and give them the injection. I'll bet when they woke up and found out they were cured they'd hug my neck and be thrilled and would start running after their friends and loved ones who needed the shot as well.

Dear One, we have the cure for everything and people are dying every day without having taken the cure. Believers have the cure of an eternity in heaven instead of in hell. We have the cure for sorrow and sadness, sin and disgrace. It will turn these symptoms into joy and peace, contentment and security. That cure is Jesus and yet do we make the cure available to everyone we know? If not, why not? Why do you care if they act like you're bugging them? They'll do the same thing, once they give up and give in to Jesus. And by the way, don't let anything they say or do to you make any difference, don't let it matter to you. You know someday they'll thank you for it and hug your neck; besides our Father God wants us to tell the world about His Son.

Read Acts Chapter 1 and focus on verse 8: But you will receive power when the Holy Spirit comes on you, and you will be my witnesses in Jerusalem, and in all Judea and Samaria, and to the ends of the earth.

Read Romans Chapter 1 and then focus on verse 16: I am not ashamed of the gospel of the gospel, because it is the power of God for the salvation of everyone who believes, for the Jew, then for the Gentile.

You Ask Me Why

You ask me why I bug you and
Then say, "I want to know."
At times you've even wanted me
To just shut up and go.

But if you only knew how much
I want what's best for you,
Perhaps you'd have a little more
Patience than you do.

I know you think that I'm a pest
And cause you too much strife.
If you were dying and I knew
That I could save your life,

I'd do anything I had to
To make you take the cure,
Even if you tried to run for
You simply were not sure.

I might have to tie you up and
Cure you against your will,
And with you kicking and screaming
Give you that shot or pill.

Then once you found that you were well
You'd come and hug my neck,
Probably say, "I'm sorry." And
I'd just say, "What the heck?"

You know you'd do the same for me
If you were in my shoes,
And exactly what I did for you
That's what you too would choose.

Well, my friend, I know and have the
Cure for every ill,
But you will find that it's not found
In any shot or pill.

Just as soon as you take the cure
Your life will start to change,
Now you'll find your priorities
You'll want to rearrange.

And suddenly you'll want to bug
Your friends as I bugged you.
Saying, "Jesus loves you," - and that...
He wants to make things new.

So now you know just why I tried
To tell you from the start,
"Don't waste another minute but...
Let Jesus into your heart."

When They All Turn Their Backs

Friend, Have you ever had a time in your life when it seemed that everything that could go wrong did and then some. You thought nothing else could go wrong but it did. Sadly, it happened to be one of those times when not a single real or supposed friend was available. The whole episode made you feel so alone, so helpless.

It can actually make you feel like your whole life is falling apart and no one even cares. It can be the loneliest feeling in the world. It can happen to Christians just like it does to the unbeliever, but the difference is that the Christian has someone to turn to that the unbeliever doesn't. Many times, it's not that our friends don't love us, or that they don't care, it's simply that they weren't available when we needed them most, but it was probably for a good reason.

There is one friend who's always there for us, never too busy to listen and to answer our prayers. Ready to comfort and encourage us regardless of our circumstance; and faithful so see us through to the other side of the situation.

No one can do for us what Jesus can and will if we call on Him during our time of need. Trust Him for everything and always remember He's there day and night and He'll never let you down. He loves you so much and wants only what's best for you.

Read Psalms 57 and then focus on verses 1-2: Have mercy on me oh, God, have mercy on me, for my soul trusteth in Thee, in the shadow of Your wings will I take my refuge until all these calamities be passed by.

Read Psalms 32 and then focus on verse 7: You are my hiding place; You will protect me from trouble and surround me with songs of deliverance.

When They All Turn Their Backs

When your heart is hurting and you
Feel it's about to break,
Then you find yourself wondering
Just how much you can take.

It seems that no one cares about
What you've been going through -
You question, "Things will never change...
So what am I to do?

When suddenly life feels as though...
It's totally gone wrong,
In your sad heart you ponder, "Oh,
Lord, where do I belong?"

You had a lot of friends until
They found you had a need,
Then when one turned away soon the
Others followed his lead.

When friends and loved ones forsake you
And leave you all alone,
They no longer come to visit,
Nor call you on the phone.

Don't be down or discouraged for
You'll find these are the facts,
The Dear Lord will still be here when...
They all turn their backs.

He'll provide for all your needs and
Never leave you alone,
When no one else calls...He will...
But He won't need a phone.

He'll whisper by His Spirit of
His great, great love for you,
And you will always find Him here
No matter what you do.

He wants you to lean on Him for...
Forever and a day.
No matter where you find yourself
It's not too far away.

He's your very best friend and He...
Knows all that you go through...
Forget those friends who turned away
They weren't real friends to you.

So remember...

You'll have living water to drink
Whenever you thirst,
And when you have a need you must
Always seek the Lord first.

Critical

Do you have a habit of criticizing those who don't dress, act, talk, walk or perhaps think the same way you do? Do you judge those people with a different standard or measuring rod than with which you would want to be judged? We really can't judge or criticize anyone. Many years ago, because I had never been prejudiced and wasn't raised in a prejudiced home, I couldn't understand anyone being that way and I couldn't tolerate it. The very thought of not loving someone due to the color of their skin was beyond my comprehension. One day I had a conversation with my pastor and he said, "Carolyn, be careful not to be prejudiced against prejudiced people." And the minute he said that I realized I was. I had no right to judge prejudice people when I had my own areas of weakness. All we can do is pray for anyone we see overtaken in a fault and not to judge. I had to ask the Lord to love prejudiced people through me; and immediately I realized that we are to love all men, even our enemies.

Sometimes a person isn't doing anything wrong, they simply don't wear the kind of clothes we do, walk or talk the way we do. Their grammar may be incorrect, but you know what, I've never found that to be a sin, anywhere in the Word of God. Have you?

I always despised tattoos and two of my grandsons have been in the Navy and both got several tattoos. At first it broke my heart, and then the Lord really impressed upon me that He's more concerned about their soul than a couple of tattoos, and besides they are both fine young men who love the Lord. Being in prison ministry has also taught me not to judge or criticize; for many inmates, not only have tattoos but most don't walk or talk the way I do, and yet the Lord has given me a great love and burden for those who are incarcerated. In fact, some have come to live with us for a while when they got out and it has always been a privilege and a blessing.

Dear One, if we'll let Him, Jesus will not only love others unconditionally through us but He will love the unlovely as well, and they need love the most. We don't want others to judge us, and we want the Lord and other people to love us unconditionally. Should we do any less?

If we waste our time and energy criticizing we might miss out on a wonderful new relationship, a great new friend. So, let's all keep a tight rein on our thoughts when it comes to others, and let's think the best of those who may not fit our preconceived idea of what they should do or be. Worry about the log in our own eye instead of the twig in theirs.

Read Romans chapter 15 and then focus on verses 1-2 : We who are strong ought to bear with the failings of the weak and not to please ourselves. Each of us should please his neighbor for his good, to build him up.

Read Romans chapter 14 and then focus on verse 1: Accept him whose faith is weak, without passing judgment on disputable matters.

Critical

When we see others who may not look
The way we think they should,
They don't wear their hair or dress
Exactly like we would.

They may not even sound the same
As we do when we talk,
Or perhaps we don't like the way
They swagger when they walk.

Some have a tongue that when they speak
It cuts just like a knife,
No matter where they go it seems
They scar another life.

Perhaps they have tattoos - that are-
All over their body,
And walk down the street with clothes
That look mighty shoddy.

At times they may use curse words and
Have a drink now and then,
But oh, my Gawd, we wouldn't dare for
"We all" know it's a sin.

God's Spirit is the only one
With a right to condemn;
So let's be quiet and listen to
The Savior of all men.

We can't worry about the twig
In someone else's eye,
When the log in our own's so big
We barely see to get by.

Our job as children of God is...
To love all men the same;
Not criticize and malign but
Bless them in Jesus' name.

I don't think God's as concerned about...
A damn, a drink or tattoo,
As with the heart of that lonely one
Who's feeling sad, and blue.

So, don't waste time being critical...
Let the Lord have control,
For those who choose to condemn
Just might lose their soul.

Let's all look for the good in those
Whom we see every day,
And say, "God bless you", to each one
As they go on their way.

If we decide to criticize, and
There is no good reason,
Our God will soon repay us all
In His time and season.

Dare to be a Daniel

Dear One, when you think you're having a bad day think about some of the saints in the old testament. A couple of good examples of how to handle tough times are Daniel and his friends, Shadrach, Meshach and Abednego. These young men were true to their God regardless of what the outcome of their faithfulness might have been. They loved the Lord so much, that if their faithfulness had caused them to lose their lives, then so be it. But as we all know the Lord honored their obedience. For Daniel he shut the lion's mouth and didn't allow it to harm him, which in turn blew the kings mind, and it was a real testimony to him of Daniel's God. And then when Daniel's friends were thrown into the furnace, the Lord actually went into the flames with them. And even though the fire became so hot that the men stoking the flames, literally fell down dead from the heat, the young men came out alive and totally unharmed. Their faith was another strong witness to their God's faithfulness.

Would our faith be strong enough to get into a cage with a lion or to get into a fiery furnace? Shouldn't we find it easy to trust the Lord through our daily trials and temptations? After all, if He created the world and the universe and everything in it and He holds it all together so perfectly, I do believe that nothing we might find ourselves called to go through could be too hard for Him to handle.

Always remember my friend, that all that the Lord did for Daniel, He'll do it for you as well, and you can rest in His arms knowing He'll meet all of your needs, and nothing is too hard for Him.

Read the book of Daniel.

Read Psalms chapter 37 and then focus on verses 3-5: Trust in the Lord and do good; dwell in the land and enjoy safe pasture. Delight yourself in the Lord and He will give you the desires of your heart. Commit your way to the Lord, trust in Him and He will bring it to pass.

Dare to be a Daniel

My friend,
Do you often feel surrounded...
With troubles on every side,
Your stress keeps getting stronger
Till you want to run and hide.

Like Daniel you must always try,
To trust your heavenly Father;
For him, the Lord, shut the lion's mouth...
So, it wasn't even a bother.

When you feel you need a friend,
They all seem to disappear;
You longingly call their names
And yet no one seems to hear.

Shadrach, Meshach and Abednego
Were thrown into the flames,
Jesus stayed there with them until...
Out of the furnace they came.

The king's men stoking the oven,
Fell down dead on the floor...
For as the fire got hotter and hotter,
They just couldn't take any more.

Trust the Lord like Daniel did
Through all of his many trials;
When temptation like a lion,
Is stalking you for miles.

Trust Him like Daniel's friends
When the flames are burning higher;
Just keep your eyes on Jesus...
And you won't be burned by the fire.

Give everything to the Savior,
All your trials and troubles sore,
And all that He did for Daniel
He'll do for you, and even more.

Has the World Gone Mad?

One day I found a website where I could post my poems and short stories and other people could sign on and read them; and I could read works posted by other writers. If you wanted to you could leave comments or suggestions for the author of the work. After a short time I felt so sad, for at times, I would read a lovely uplifting spiritual poem by a particular poet and think what a blessing, so I would check again for their next posting. It was so disappointing, that many times the very same person who wrote the wonderful, uplifting Christian poem had written something that after a couple of lines I had to quit reading due to the content, which was anything but Christian. Some works by these same people I couldn't even begin to read them for they actually had warnings at the beginning about sexual or erotic content or vulgar language.

I emailed these people asking if it wasn't inconsistent and inappropriate for Christians to write in a godly way one day and the next in such a worldly way. Well, you can imagine the responses I received. I was being legalistic and that there's nothing wrong with eroticism. Although I wrote these writers and said the world gives us the freedom of expression to write that way but as a Christian, do we write to build others up or to tear them down? Do we write to glorify God or to receive the praises of men?

Many writers think if they don't use sexual content, profanity and vulgar language they won't sell their books, so they give in to the world's way of thinking. The saying garbage in and garbage out is so true and what good can come from a person reading and thus taking in erotic, gory, hateful, mean or violent material? Everyone but especially Christians should use their gifts and talents for the glory of God and to be a blessing to others, that's why the Lord gave us our particular gifts. Don't misuse them or you could lose them.

Read Philippians Chapter 4 and then focus on verses 8-9: Finally brothers, whatever is true, whatever is noble, whatever is right, whatever is pure, whatever is lovely, whatever is admirable - if anything is excellent or praiseworthy, think about such things; and whatever you have learned or received, heard or seen in me - put it into practice, and the God of peace will be with you.

Read Philippians Chapter 2 and then focus on verses 3-4: Do nothing out of selfish ambition or vain conceit but in humility consider others as more important they yourselves. Each of you should look not only to your own interest, but also to the interest of others.

Has the World Gone Mad?

At times it breaks my heart to read
What's written on the page,
Although the words were penned by some
Well-known poetic sage.

If what I read comes from the mind
Of a human being,
Sometimes I can't believe the words
That my eyes are seeing.

It's one thing to express ourselves
When feeling sad and low,
Or even when life may seem to be
A heavy load we tow.

What is it when the words we read
Are just plain filth and gore?
Sometimes it gives the reader chills
Right to their body's core.

We may have the freedom to write...
Whatever comes to mind,
But when others read our work...
How will it be defined?

There're good ways to write a story
A poem, script or song,
Yet many try to make it seem
Like doing right is wrong.

They think no one will read their work
Without profanity,
And feel that to refrain would be
Complete insanity.

At times I have to ask myself,
"Has the world gone mad?"
No matter where you turn things are
So evil, sick or sad.

Our world needs to go back to when
Doing right was what to do,
Somehow we lost our way, my friend,
I'm going back won't you.

Let's all hold hands and take a stand
Then try to do what's right;
If we should slip, don't just quit, or
Go down without a fight.

Instead let's lift each other up
Find ways to show we care,
And use our gift of writing as
A blessing we can share.

I'll Give and I'll Take

Dear One, have you ever thought about how much our Savior gives, and how much we take? And how much He takes and we give. If you'll take the time to do that, I'm sure it will amaze you.

Our precious, wonderful Jesus, gives us everything good in life and all the negatives He removes from our lives and willingly takes them upon Himself. He takes our sadness and gives us His joy, He'll take all our losses and turn them to gains. All you can do is thank Him for He wants nothing in return. I don't think our finite minds can truly fathom the extent of what He has truly done for us, far beyond giving His life for our salvation.

One important thing He did for us is that He left us His example to pattern our lives after. What a great blessing for it leaves us no rhyme or reason for not knowing what to do or how to live.

Friend, don't take the Lord's goodness for granted but seriously think about the enormity of it all.

Read Romans Chapter 12 and focus on verses 1-2:Therefore, I beseech you, brothers, in view of God's mercy, to offer your bodies as living sacrifices, holy and pleasing to God - this is your spiritual act of worship(reasonable service -in the King James). Do not conform any longer to the pattern of this world, but be transformed by the renewing of your mind.

Also focus on verses 9-10: Love must be sincere. Hate what is evil; cling to what is good. Be devoted to one another in brotherly love, Honor one another above yourselves.

I'll Give and I'll Take

Jesus says, "I love you, My child
I'll gladly take your pain,
Then suffer your losses...
And I'll give you My gain.

Just because I love you,
I'll bear all your sorrow,
So, when you have a need...
You won't need to borrow.

I'll also take your poverty,
And give you My wealth.
I'll suffer your sickness,
Then give you good health.

I'll take away your grief,
And I'll give you my joy,
So, from now on sorrow,
You will never employ.

I gave you My life...and then you,
Gladly gave me your death.
Now, you'll be in heaven,
When you take your last breath.

I'll bear life's storms for you,
The strong wind and the rain,
It's blue skies and sunshine,
When you call on My name.

Dear One, I'll always meet your need
No matter what the cost,
And now that you've been found,
You can never be lost.

I'll never, ever leave you,
But I'll give and I'll take,
And all the things I've done,
I've done just for your sake."

The Flower of Life

Think about it, life is like a flower, and the Lord created both to bring beauty into the world. It's truly amazing, when you think of how many different shapes, colors and sizes of flowers there are and how each one is totally unique. And no matter where the flower is: in a vase in the house, in a beautiful garden, along the highway, or in a weed patch they still add so much beauty to the place where they're on display. They may seem to show up even more in a weed patch for there they stand out from everything around them.

I believe our lives are just the same way, where ever we are we should stand out from all those around us. We should be different and we should add even more to our surroundings the worse they might be.   The Lord planted us where He wanted us to bloom, and where He knew we could add beauty to the lives of all who happen to pass by. If we are in a weed patch, then the Lord knew that weed patch needed some beauty in it. If the beauty of a flower can make people smile and brighten their day; then it seems like we should have the same effect wherever we go - making people smile and feel happy.

The big difference in our beauty and the beauty of a flower is that ours should be Jesus Christ shining through us. We should be radiating His beauty to those around us. With so much ugliness in the world it desperately needs some beauty to brighten up things a little. Will you be a flower in the Garden of life or a weed that needs to be plucked up and tossed into the fire? The choice is up to you!

Read Matthew Chapter 5 and then focus on verses 14-15: You are the light of the world. A city on a hill cannot be hidden. Neither do people light a lamp and put it under a bowl. Instead they put it on its stand, and it gives light to everyone in the house. In the same way, let your light shine before men, that they may see your good deeds and praise your Father in heaven.

If you are a flower in the garden of life and not a weed, let your beauty (good works) shine for those around you to see. Be the blessing that your Father wants you to be.

Read II Corinthians Chapter 6 and then focus on verse 17: Therefore come out from among them and be ye separate says the Lord.

The Flower of Life

Just like a beautiful flower
Life goes from bud to bloom,
It's woven like a tapestry,
On God's own special loom.

The petals soon begin to droop,
They quickly get that way;
The flower's open just awhile,
Then it withers away.

When the lovely blooms are open,
The way God has them made,
They bring delight to everyone
Before they start to fade.

We should bring such awesome beauty
Into the lives of those nearby,
That like the bloom of the flower
We will bless each passerby.

If a pretty little blossom
Grows up in a briar patch,
It has a special beauty that
A weed could never match.

Flowers never blend in with weeds,
They stand out all alone,
Even if they're the only flower
The weed patch has ever grown.

Do we stand out from this world or...
Blend right in with the crowd?
Do we bring a ray of Son-shine
Or a dark foreboding cloud?

Have we brought joy to the world or
Salvation to the lost?
Have we shared and cared for others,
No matter what the cost?

When all our time on earth is gone,
It's time for us to go
Will we leave a special fragrance...
And some sweet afterglow?

When our hair has turned to silver
Our days are all gone by,
Will Jesus say, "Well done, My Child!"
When we meet Him in the sky?

Come Home

Friend, in your lifetime, have you ever wandered away from the Lord? I wish I could say that I had never had that happen, and yet in my heart I know it has. May be not for a really long period of time but long enough to realize it's no fun. And I was old enough in the Lord to know better. I still said my prayers and went to church, but in my heart I knew I wasn't living the life the Lord wanted me to live.

Nothing this world has to offer is worth wandering away from our close relationship with the Lord. Regardless of how small or insignificant the thing might seem, if it's going to interrupt our fellowship with our wonderful Savior, run from it. For what ever it might have to offer, it can not compare to the blessings we have in Jesus. It may bring a moment of temporary pleasure but it will never bring you any lasting joy or happiness.

Why would we ever begin to think that there is anything better than perfection, and why would we settle for less? Can you imagine anyone trading in a diamond for a cubic zirconium; it simply wouldn't make any sense.

Christian, if you wandered away from the Lord, days, weeks, months or even years ago, He's waiting with open arms for you to come back home. Please, don't put it off, tomorrow may never come.

Read James Chapter 5 and then focus on verse 19: My brothers, if one of you should wander from the truth and someone should bring him back, remember this: Whoever turns a sinner from the error of his way will save him from death and cover over a multitude of sins.

Read I Timothy chapter 6 and then focus on verses 10-12: Some people, eager for money, have wandered from the faith and pierced themselves with many griefs. But you oh, man of God, flee from all this, and pursue righteousness, godliness, , faith, love, endurance and gentleness. Fight the good fight of faith.

Come Home

It's never too late to turn back to the Lord,
You may be eighteen or eighty, one hundred or ten.
He's waiting to receive you with arms open wide,
Back into the family again.

He'll never remember the times in your past,
So don't let your heart be dismayed;
He only cares that His child has come home,
Your reunion...no longer delayed.

If you'll turn around right where you are,
You'll find Jesus leading the way;
The way back to joy and fellowship sweet,
The way back from night into day.

You may have spent years, many years,
Living in the very vilest of sins
But the past won't matter one bit, my friend,
When your new life with Jesus begins.

His voice has ever been calling you,
"Come back to your family and friends;
You've been gone quite a while, but
You'll be back forever, and forever never ends".

Please don't waste another minute
Living out there on your own;
Turn around and take His hand,
Let Him lead you back home.

The angels in heaven will be singing,
They'll be shouting with great joy;
Over the long awaited return of
That man, woman, girl or boy.

With even one child missing,
The family just isn't complete;
Songs don't ring as loudly,
The fellowship's not as sweet.

My dear friend, please come home,
Hurry and don't try to delay;
Tomorrow may never come
So, turn around and come right away.

Forget the Past

Dear Child of God, we all have our own sin problems and we should let the Lord help us to have victory over them in our lives. But if and when you are overtaken in a fault, immediately confess that sin to the Lord and move on. We all know I John 1:9 says that if we confess our sins, He is faithful and just to forgive us of our sins and to cleanse us from all unrighteousness.

Sadly many times even when we have confessed our sins and moved on, that old devil, continues on and on reminding us of what we did wrong. Even though the Lord has forgiven us, we start worrying about what we said or did and it seems we're not able to forgive ourselves. Our thoughts are one of the devil's favorite places to attack and we must tell him, "Get thee behind me Satan, you have no power over me." (And he doesn't, unless we freely chose to give it to him.

If we know the Lord has forgiven us, should we not forgive ourselves? At times we may need to be reminded of God's forgiveness and at other times we may need to remind someone else who is living under such a heavy burden as well, and one that's totally unnecessary.

Read Psalms chapter 103 and then focus on verses 8-13: The Lord is compassionate and gracious, slow to anger, abounding in love. He will not always accuse, nor will He harbor His anger forever; He does not treat us as our sins deserve or repay us according to our iniquities. For as high as the heavens are above the earth, so great is His love for those who fear Him As far as the east is from the west, so far has He removed our transgressions from us.

Forget the Past

There are those times we get caught up
In worrying about our sin;
Then the devil gets excited
Although this war he'll never win.

He delights when he makes us start
To worry and to fret;
By constantly reminding us,
Of all the sins we should forget.

Whenever we confess our sins
The Lord remembers them no more;
But Satan brings them to our minds
In his loud ear-splitting roar.

It's then that we should blot him out
And put our fingers in our ears;
For he often will continue
Until we find ourselves in tears.

But the Bible says resist him
And eventually he'll flee;
So speak the word and stomp your feet
And very soon, my friend you'll see...

You don't need to worry about
Any thing that is in your past;
Although old Satan may get loud his
Snorting and roaring just won't last.

And yesterday you must forget
To reach for all that lies ahead;
Things in the past we cannot change
So we should count each one as dead.

For there's no sense in worrying
About time we wasted once before;
But from now on let's do those things
That bless others more and more.

In the future when we err...we must...
Confess, our sin and then move on;
For why hold on to what the Lord
Says He considers to be gone?

I'm Ready Now

If you knew the Lord was coming soon, what would your thoughts and attitude be? Would you be rejoicing, excited and looking forward to that moment, or would you be dreading its coming? I hope that just the thought of being at home with the Lord is uplifting and exciting to you. If it's not it definitely should be and if it's not why not? What would cause you to be apprehensive?

The thought of leaving our loved ones is a little bit melancholy for we'll miss them until we're together again. But there's always the wonderful possibility that the Rapture could come before the Lord takes us through death; then all of our friends and loved ones who know Jesus as their Savior will be going with us. What a joy that would be!

My prayer for you my friend, is that you will reach a point in your Christian life, where you can be at peace with the thought of death, the thought of going to your real home to be with your Father God, your Savior, the Lord Jesus and all your friends and loved ones who are already in heaven waiting for you.

This should be an event that every believer looks forward to and although they don't want to rush it neither do they dread, or want to delay it. We'll all experience dying grace when the time comes and until then we don't need it. You might say that the Lord comes to carry us home, and He won't come to get us before our time. And we can rest in the fact that His timing is always perfect.

Read I Thessalonians Chapter 4 and then focus on verses 16-18: For the Lord Himself shall descend from heaven with a shout, with the voice of the archangel and the trumpet call of God, and the dead in Christ will rise first and then those who are alive and remain, shall be caught up together with them in the clouds to meet the Lord in the air, and so shall we ever be with the Lord.

Read Psalms Chapter 116 and then focus on verse 15: Precious in the sight of the Lord is the death of His saints.

I'm Ready Now

Father, I'm all ready now and
There's something that I know,
No need to pack my bags although
It's time for me to go.

I've had a wonderful life here
Some things I hate to leave,
Like all those whom I love, Dear Lord
And please don't let them grieve.

They knew someday we'd have to part
Until they too shall come,
I guess it's only natural...
That they would miss me some.

I told them all to celebrate
The day that I depart,
And although I'll be in heaven
I'll still be in their heart.

They all need to remember that
I'm going home to God,
My temporary tent is all
That's put beneath the sod.

I can't believe at last it's time
For me to say goodbye,
And soon I'll be arriving in
That land beyond the sky.

I think I see You coming now
And I can hardly wait,
To see my friends and loved ones
Who are waiting at the gate.

Yes, Lord, I'm all ready and my
Redemption draweth nigh.
Any moment I'll be leaving...
For the sweet by and by.

He's Only a Prayer Away

Dear Saint of God, it always hurts us to see someone we love going through suffering of any kind. It may be a spiritual, physical, mental, emotional or financial problem, but what ever it is we never want to see those people that we care so much about going through anything that we can't take away or make it better.

If we know Jesus as our Savior we do have a lot of relief within our reach to offer to those who need help, healing or encouragement and we should be ready at all times to offer that help.

There are times that the Lord will use us in some capacity to minister to   that friend or loved one, but there are those times when He may want them to turn to Him, but unless they know the Lord they won't know how to have a relationship with Him. In that case, it is our responsibility to lead them to a saving knowledge of the Lord Jesus Christ.

You sometimes have a situation where the person knows the Lord but they just need to be reminded that He cares and that He's the answer to the question and the solution to the problem they might have. Nothing is too hard for the Lord to take care of it. No problem too hard to solve and no question to hard to answer.

So friend, be ready at all times to let our friends or loved ones (or even a stranger who needs the Lord), know that Jesus is only a prayer away.

Read Philippians Chapter 4 and then focus on verse 13: I can do everything through him who gives me strength.

Read verse 19: And my God will meet all your needs according to his glorious riches in Christ Jesus.

Read I Thessalonians Chapter 5 and then focus on verses 16- 18: Be joyful always; pray continually; give thanks in all circumstances, for this is God's will for you in Christ Jesus

He's Only a Prayer Away

My friend, it breaks my heart to see
You're hurting and in pain.
Life seems like a storm and you've been
Caught out in the rain.

I know you're really hurting and
It makes me, oh, so sad...
To know someone so dear to me
Is really feeling bad.

When you find you've lost your way,
And you're feeling alone;
The people all around you seem...
As cold as a stone.

I can only say, "I love you."
And let you know I care,
Still in your heart you've questioned,
"Just how much you can bear?"

I know a place where you'll be safe,
From all the stress and strife;
In Jesus' arms there's peace that'll last...
All the days of your life.

I wish that I could take you
But all that I can do,
Is point the way to the Savior...
He'll always see you through.

You've been longing for a stronghold
Where you can feel secure,
Well, the Lord is the answer and
Of that you can be sure.

From now on remember....

When you think you're not able
To go on another day
Get on your knees - go to Jesus
He's only a prayer away.

I Take the Blame

I honestly believe that when we sin, we always know it, although we may have done it on the spur of the moment and perhaps unintentionally, we still know it. It may have been something that we feel was completely insignificant but we must remember a sin is a sin.

Then there are those of us who don't want to take responsibility for our actions, so we jokingly say, "The devil made me do it!" or we try to rationalize and blame someone else. We say, "If Carolyn wouldn't have done that I wouldn't have done this." But you know I've never read a scripture that says because someone else did something wrong it makes it okay for me to do something wrong as well. Sometimes we, say she

(fill in the blank) so I had the right to do what I did. Again, I don't believe you'll find a scripture to back that up.

To have a right relationship with the Lord we must own up to our sin, confess it, repent of it and ask Him to help us to have victory over it. The Holy Spirit will convict us of our sin, if we want to listen, and if we do, soon we'll find ourselves being convicted before we commit the sin.

That still small voice will warn us even before we say or do something displeasing to our Father. We have the free will to listen to and obey that voice or to shut our ears to it. Hopefully my friend, you'll want the Holy Spirit to help you be victorious over any sin in your life and all you have to do is say, "Lord, please let your wonderful Holy Spirit convict me of any known or unknown sin in my life. And give me the strength to be victorious over any sin you reveal to me. In Jesus Name I pray, Amen"

Read: I John Chapter 1 and focus on verse 9: If we confess our sin, He is faithful and just to forgive us of our sin and to cleanse us from all unrighteousness.

Verse 8: If we claim to be without sin, we deceive ourselves and the truth is not in us.

I Take the Blame

Can you honestly say...

Guess what, Lord, at last I can say,
"My blinded eyes now see,"
I'm the one to blame and I'm just
Guilty as I can be.

In my heart I used to think - when
I sin I'm not to blame,
It must have been somebody else -
For I felt no real shame.

It always seemed so easy to
Point fingers at another,
Strangers and friends - or at times a
Sister or a brother.

Carrying all the blame alone
Well, it was just too tough,
And sharing simply made it seem
It wasn't quite as rough.

But Lord, at last you reached inside
That place that's deep within,
Where I always did my utmost
To try and hide my sin.

Now what can I do - You've placed it
Right in front of my eyes,
All that ugliness and sin I
So loathe and despise?

Father, I must now confess it
And even take the blame,
For I don't want my life to go on

Being just the same.
From now on all those ugly sins
That you can see in me,
I must quickly own up to and
Admit wholeheartedly.

For I don't want a single thing
To come between us two,
That might keep one of my prayers
From getting through to You.

My Heart on Paper

Dear One, the Lord has blessed you with certain gifts, such as teaching, evangelism, helps and the list goes on, but you may be gifted in one or more areas. The thing we must always remember is that our Father gives us these gifts to use for His glory and to be a blessing to others, both believers and unbelievers. Some Christians never even find out what their gift or gifts are and thus they are never used and the Lord may give them to someone else, who will use them for Him.

Along with our gifts, comes the responsibility of using them wisely, not misusing them. A person with the gift of evangelism might be an excellent sales person in their regular employment; and they could misuse their ability of persuasion to over sell people or to sell people something they really can't afford. Hopefully, their compassion will help them have the desire to meet needs and do what's best for others.

It is such a privilege to be given these gifts and we need to take the responsibility very seriously. If you have been given the gift of writing, then please, use it to be a blessing to your readers and to bring glory and honor to your Father. For if you are seeking to write in that manner then you are writing led of the Spirit and you are letting yourself be the pen and the Lord Himself is the author of your work. So it removes any pride for you didn't come up with that poem or story, your Father did, and all the praise belongs to Him. Isn't that really awesome, I think so, that way we can't get puffed up with that ugly old pride.

Read Romans Chapter 11 and then focus on verse 29: For the gifts and calling of God are without repentance.

Read I Corinthians chapter 14 and then focus on verse 12: Even so ye, forasmuch as ye are zealous of spiritual gifts, seek that ye may excel to the edifying of the church.

My Heart on Paper

Poetry's my heart on paper;
And it reveals my soul.
Is it sheer reality or
Simply playing a role?

I may write of joy or sadness,
Sometimes sickness or health,
A blessing or perhaps a curse,
One's poverty or wealth.

Some writers make it scary but...
I write of peace and calm,
Sadly some want horror and gore,
I want a soothing balm...

My poems are an overflow
Of the joy within my heart,
And when I pick up my pen
That's where I like to start.

So, I try my best to listen
To God's Holy Spirit,
It tells me what to write but I
Must be still to hear it.

I want to encourage your heart
If you've been feeling blue...
So sometimes my poem or story,
Will share what I've been through.

At times my words may tell you what...
The Lord has done for me;
Or how He can heal the sick and...
Then cause the blind to see.

I want to write what God can use
To glorify His name,
As others read it may they find
They'll never be the same.

There's only one reason to write
A poem or a story,
That's to make the Savior smile and
Give Him all the glory.

If my poem's a blessing to
Someone along my way,
Please, give the praises to the Lord,
Is all that I can say.

So Many Sad Faces

Have you noticed that every where you go today there are so many sad faces? When you go out to dinner with your family or friends, there aren't nearly as many people smiling and laughing at the other tables as there used to be. Many look as though their face would crack if they tried to smile. There are times you want to say something thoughtful to someone at another table, simply because they look as though they are so lonely and sad, especially the ones sitting by themselves.

There are people from all walks of life - every segment of society - who are desperately trying to find, love, joy, peace, happiness and contentment in their lives. They don't realize that what they are seeking will not be found in acquiring more and more material possessions, drugs or alcohol, fame or fortune, and not only that but sadly they're looking in all the wrong places.

There is no one without Christ who will ever find what they want until first they find Him. They don't realize that every heart has a hole in it that only Jesus can fill. And once that hole is filled when they start seeking His will instead of their own, He'll provide all the other things they need in order to be happy.

Those who know the way should joyfully point these lonely people in the right direction, in order for them to find that for which they've been searching. If we'll just ask the Lord to open the door for us to have the opportunity to help these sad people find their way, He will gladly grant our requests, probably in abundance due to the number of lonely people.

Read Matthew Chapter 6 and then focus on verses 28-34: "And why do you worry about clothes? See how the lilies of the field grow. They do not labor or spin. Yet I tell you that not even Solomon in all his splendor was dressed like one of these. If that is how God clothes the grass of the field, which is here today and tomorrow is thrown into the fire, will he not much more clothe you, O you of little faith? So do not worry, saying, 'What shall we eat?' or 'What shall we drink?' or 'What shall we wear?' For the pagans run after all these things, and your heavenly Father knows that you need them. But seek first his kingdom and his righteousness, and all these things will be given to you as well. Therefore do not worry about tomorrow, for tomorrow will worry about itself. Each day has enough trouble of its own.

So Many Sad Faces

Whenever I look around it seems
I can't help but see,
Terribly sad faces always
Looking right back at me.

It breaks my heart to know there are
So many lonely souls,
Some may have a lot of money
But still their shoes have holes.

They may have their name in lights
Yet tears are in their eyes,
And the life that they've been living
It's really only lies

All the fame and fortune cannot
Fill up their empty hearts,
Becoming a child of the King
Is where that filling starts.

God loves His children so much -
He gives them blessings galore,
His storehouse never runs dry
There's always plenty more.

Many will spend their entire life
Looking for the answer,
They may be some business tycoon
An actor or a dancer.

They'll look and look but never find
It's always the wrong place,
What they seek is only found by
God's amazing grace.

The happiness the world can give
Won't ever last for long,
If they'll seek the joy of the Lord
They'll find they can't go wrong.

The world and its ways can never
Offer them joy and peace,
But if they'll turn to the Savior
Their blessings will never cease.

I've Been There All Along

Dear One, do you realize that our Father is there for us from beginning to end. He brings us into this world and He is there when we leave.

Sadly, there are some He has to tell, they can't enter into heaven, but it doesn't mean He didn't love them, for the Lord sends no one to hell, all who go, send themselves.

As His children, we may stray away like the prodigal son, but we never stray so far that He doesn't know where we are. When we get tired of wandering around in no-man's land, we can go back home and be welcomed with open arms. Wherever we are our Father is always as close as the mention of His name.

When we are a child of the King, in a moment of weakness we might lose our faith, and yet scripture tells us He will still be faithful to us.

If we refuse our Father's help it may interrupt our communication but not our relationship. We may turn our back on Him but He will never turn His back on us.

We are all truly, so blessed - blessed beyond our ability to comprehend.

Read II Timothy Chapter 2 and then focus on verses 11-13: Here is a trustworthy saying: If we died with Him, we will also live with Him; If we endure, we will also reign with Him. If we disown Him, He will also disown us; if we are faithless, He will remain faithful, for He cannot disown Himself.

The Lord knows us even when we don't know ourselves.

I've Been There All Along

My child, I love you so and I've been there by your side...
Since the day that you were born; and that cannot be denied.

You were just a tiny baby...I guarded you with all my might;
I never left you for a minute; I was with you day and night.

Yes, I was unseen - but with you - even though you didn't know,
I stayed right there close beside you, so I could watch you grow.

When you became a wee toddler I followed you around,
You never saw or heard me for I didn't make a sound

Soon you became a teen, and "I don't need God" you said.
Still I didn't leave, although you told others I was dead.

At twenty you called my name and begged me to let you live,
After your wreck - a dire report - the doctors had to give.

Once your body mended - you surrendered your life to me;
And I poured out the blessings; you thought you'd never see.

At twenty-five you married - the great girl I sent your way;
And you and your sweet wife have been a blessing since that day.

Next in life you had a little girl and boy of your own,
And although they'll keep me busy, much too soon they'll both be grown

Now don't ever forget, whether your faith is weak or strong
I'm by your side forever and I've been there all along.

Misunderstood

Friend, have there been times that you walked away from a situation and you felt as if you had left things at a level where either your words, actions or both were misunderstood?

Maybe you've had a boss or a friend, that somehow misinterpreted something you said or did and you really never had the opportunity to explain yourself. And the sad thing is you were right in what you said or did but you were totally misunderstood. It leaves you thinking, "Why, Lord? I try so hard to say and do the right thing, because I want to be a good witness for you, but it just seems like the harder I try the more I find myself misunderstood."

Well, remember the devil does his best to try and blow our witness. Nothing makes him happier. So many times it's not what we say or do but how that other person hears or perceives it. It can be so aggravating. The only thing we can do is leave it in the hands of the Lord, for He's the one person who knows the truth and thankfully He's the only one that really matters.

All we can do is ask the Lord to help us say and do things in a way that can't be misunderstood, but in a way that will always be pleasing to Him. Leave it in the Lord's hands and forgive those who are too quick in judging what others say and do, besides, they shouldn't be judging to begin with; but once you leave it in the hands of the Lord, leave it there and don't worry about it.

Read Luke chapter 6 and then focus on verses 27-28 & 37: But I tell you who hear me: Love your enemies, do good to those who hate you, bless those who curse you, pray for those who mistreat you.

Do not judge and you will not be judged. Do not condemn, and you will not be condemned. Forgive and you will be forgiven. Give, and it will be given to you.

Read Proverbs Chapter 16 and then focus on verse 23: A wise man's heart guides his tongue.

Misunderstood

Why is it there are times that I
Feel so misunderstood?
I try my best to do what's right
Yet things just aren't too good.

And Lord, I know while You were here
You were so mistreated;
But in the war with Satan, He's
The one that got defeated.

They spit on You and beat Your back
Until Your flesh was shredded;
But the day that You were crucified, You
Knew where You were headed.

The times You fought the devil...You
Never lost a battle,
And with each shout of victory the
Gates of hell You'd rattle.

In my life You're the only One
Who truly knows the facts,
And all the things I say or do,
To You adds or detracts.

Since I am Your ambassador
You must be seen in me.
When people look my way it's You
That they should always see.

Help me do things in a way that
Can't be misunderstood,
And do them just exactly as
The Bible says I should.

Then when the world calls out my name
With all of its demands.
I will leave the situation
Completely in Your hands,

So, if someone misunderstands,
Now there's no need to worry,
I'll tell them that You're in control
And quit judging in a hurry.

Lines and Creases

When I was young I always thought, I would never have a face lift, and I thought people were just worrying about the small stuff in life if they said they wanted plastic surgery, trying to look younger. Little did I know that at about the age of fifty I would start pulling my loose skin on my neck and cheeks back with my fingers and I would think, "Gee, this sure would make me look more refreshed and maybe even a little younger. " And then I'd forget all about it.

I can't say that as time has progressed that I haven't thought about it again, for I have definitely thought about it when someone I know has had one and they look so good. But I've decided, that for me, I feel like my lines and creases all came from laughing or crying and usually from

weeping tears of joy, compassion or caring. So, after thinking it over I felt strongly that this is the face the Lord gave me; and even though I was in a serious car wreck as a teenager, that left a scar from the corner of my eyebrow up into my hairline about two inches, I'll just keep this face with every line and crease.

I see no problem with anyone else having a facelift and especially if it's necessary to correct a birth defect or disfigurement from an accident of some kind. And I still have a fleeting thought of it myself when I look in the mirror and pull up my turkey neck. I'll bet you know what I mean.

Read Philippians chapter 4 and then focus on verse 11-12: I have learned to be content whatever the circumstances. I know what it is to be in need, and I know what it is to have plenty. I have learned the secret of being content in any and every situation.

Lines and Creases

I've tried it all...you name it, friend,
The masks, the oils, the creams,
Yet mirrors don't reflect the face
That I see in my dreams.

Light moisturizers for the day
And heavy for the night
With cleansers I must wash my face
But then I look a fright.

I wear make-up on my face to
Try and hide the creases,
My desire for a facelift
Seems it never ceases.

But my feeling is that if I
Go to see a surgeon,
When I wake up I'll find myself
Looking like a sturgeon.

I guess it's okay to have my
Make-up a little bit bolder,
For the age of sixty-two
I am a little older.

But I might as well keep this face
The Lord chose just for me
And looking in the mirror quit
Complaining at what I see.

For most of my lines came from
Laughing or from weeping,
So I think that makes my face a
Little more worth keeping.

Next time I look in the mirror
I'll try not to complain
Since I decided all my lines
And creases will remain.

Shout

Believer, have you ever been so excited about knowing Jesus; being a child of the King, that you wanted to shout? Have you ever been driving down the road; praying or simply thinking about how blessed you've been, and how thrilled you are, due to the fact that you have been adopted into the family of Almighty God, and you came to the point of breaking out with shouts of Hallelujah! Praise the Lord?

If you haven't, I wish you could, for it is such a wonderful feeling. It makes all the cares of the world dim and fade away for a little while. You can't praise the Lord and stay down. In my first book, "Reflections of His Love", I wrote that you can praise your hurts away and you can. It's impossible to stay down when you focus on nothing but good, uplifting things. So, friend, walking through your house or riding in your car, if you haven't done it before, break loose and give it a try. Soon you'll see what a joy it is and you'll see what you've been missing.

You'll actually receive a little taste of heaven.

I wish I could be there and do it with you!

It's awesome!

Read Hebrews chapter 13 and then focus on verse 15: Through Jesus, therefore, let us continually offer to God a sacrifice of praise - the fruit of lips that confess His name.

Read Psalms chapter 33 and then focus on verse 1: It is fitting for the upright to praise Him.

Psalms chapter 34 and focus on verse 1: His praise will always be on my lips.

Shout

Have you been redeemed by God's Holy lamb;
Are you a child of the King...the Great I Am?

Stand up and shout it so the world will know;
And go search for the lost both high and low.

Since their eyes are blind and they just can't see;
He'll shine His saving light through you and me.

When He finds that lost one He'll show them the way;
Turn their darkest night to the brightest day.

So, if you know Jesus,

My friend, you must be bold, stand up and shout!
The world needs to know what it's all about.

Jesus,

Gives joy and peace to the lonely and sad;
A special family like they've never had.

There's a soothing balm for those who are ill;
An empty cupboard He will quickly fill.

He will easily break the prisoner's chains;
Take the poor man's losses and turn them to gains.

With faith and hope He will always replace,
Nagging fear and doubt and any disgrace.

So, shout from the housetops, "Jesus is Lord!"
"He died to save us", it says in His Word.

Such a great gift you can't keep to yourself,
Don't keep it inside - like it's in a box on the shelf.

Even though He knows we foolishly sin,
If we let Him fight our battles - He won't fail to win.

All of these blessings come wrapped up in love,
Sent to His children from His throne up above.

Something's Not Right

Over the years my job transferred me many times and one of the most difficult things I always had to do, was to leave my church and friends each time I had to move, especially knowing I probably wouldn't see them again this side of heaven. The next thing I had to do was start looking for a new church in the city where I was moving. Sometimes, I would have to visit several before finding the one where I felt the Lord was leading me to join.

I always felt so uncomfortable when visiting a church that was too stuffy and stiff. They looked down their noses at anyone who walked in dressed in a way that didn't meet the church's standards, not necessarily a suit but too shabby for those fine folks. And then the being told to get up and walk around and greet people, and you could see some people being totally avoided, and the ones who received the handshakes the people looked like they hated being told to do this. It was just a situation where the greetings were much too artificial and insincere.

I personally prefer a church with its priorities straight and that loves the lost, and everyone for that matter. A church that teaches the truth of the Word of God and then the congregation applies the teachings to their daily lives. One where everyone is welcome, even that vagrant off the street. Not the one where all the pious people are looking down their nose at those who come in and don't measure up to their standards.

Dear One, never be a part of that, for what good thing does it do for the kingdom of God? To me it simply gives churches and Christians a bad name.

Read Matthew Chapter 18 and then focus on verse 10: See that you do not look down on one of these little ones. For I tell you that their angels in heaven always see the face of my Father in heaven.

Read Mark Chapter 7 and focus on verses 6-8: These people honor me with their lips, but their hearts are far from me. They worship me in vain; their teachings are but rules taught by men.

Read Luke Chapter 14 and then focus on verses 13-14: When you have a banquet, invite the poor, the crippled, the lame, the blind, and you will be blessed. Although they cannot repay you, you will be repaid at the resurrection of the righteous.

Something's Not Right

You can see the sky is blue,
And the sun shines bright,
Yet in this world
Something's not right.

There's a soft gentle breeze,
It carries puffs of white clouds,
But there's death in the air,
And it's falling on the crowds.

When you're walking in the forest
You can hear the babbling brook,
But walking down the street,
Faces have a forlorn look.

Preacher's in church, preaching the word,
The choir's singing their hymns;
Then there's the congregation
Standing in their sins.

They're looking oh so pious,
Right down their nose;
At the fellow who just walked in,
In his worn-out clothes.

Where's the care and concern,
For that lost soul?
There are walking dead among us,
And they're in Satan's control.

The love for our brother,
Who might've lost his way,
Care for the walking wounded,
Not tomorrow but today.

We're spiritually alive,
Yet act like we're dead.
We're children of the King,
Who walk around like paupers instead.

We really dread...taking the time,
To simply offer a hand.
Someone might take us up on it,
Then where would we stand?

Lord, break us and make us,
Into vessels You can use.
Never allow us,
Your gifts to misuse.

Help us to see people's needs,
And not sit idly by;
Then to allow You to use us
And never ask why.

Inside Out

Stop and think about it my friend, there's a saying that goes, "Garbage in and garbage out."And no truer words were ever spoken. This is especially true when it comes to a person's life, and it all boils down to the decisions and choices we make. For whatever we take in, is what is going to come out. If a person has their priorities in order they will be taking in the Word of God, good Bible teaching from great Bible teachers, praying throughout the day, memorizing scriptures, fellowshipping with other Christians and ministering to other people. It's also good to know your spiritual gifts so that you can use them to bless others and to glorify the Lord.

Scripture says: "you rejoice in your boastings, such rejoicing is evil...that to him that knoweth to do good and doeth it not it is sin unto him."

We wonder why there is so much evil in the world, and yet look at what is available to people, starting out - even for children - on computers, violent games, movies and television programs and sexual content every where you look, in every ad between programs on the T.V.. "Why is all this happening?" we question, and yet we have set idly by and let it happen.

The devil has a way of subtly sneaking things in before we realize it and when we do, we still do nothing to change things. If we do nothing we have no right to complain, so Christians unite and start by voting your convictions and making a stand for what's right, at every opportunity that becomes available.

** Read Philippians Chapter 4 and although I have referred to this same scripture passage several times, I highly recommend that you memorize it for it is appropriate for so many situations.

Verses 8-9: Finally brothers, whatsoever is true, whatsoever is noble, whatsoever is right, whatsoever is pure, whatsoever is lovely, whatsoever is admirable - if anything is excellent or praiseworthy—think about such things. Whatever you have learned or received, heard or seen in me - put it into practice and the God of peace will be with you.

Inside Out

There is an old saying and it's
One everyone knows,
Although it's true - few apply it
But then that's how it goes.

Most people know what they should do
But some don't really care,
They're going to do their own thing;
Give advice? You don't dare.!

Whatever goes in soon comes out,
So, do be careful my friend,
For those who take in the right things
Will find peace in the end.

We are free to use our lives as
A blessing or a curse,
What we choose to let in
Makes them better or worse.

We must take in good things since we
Live from the inside out,
And by taking in God's Word it
Leaves us no room for doubt.

For in the Word you find answers
To the problems in life,
All the directions are there
To remove sin and strife.

There's abundant joy there to ease
All your sadness and pain,
It's the place the heavy-laden
Always find sweet refrain.

God gave us directions to have
A life filled with love,
And they're found in His Word
Which He sent from above.

Yes, the Lord sent us His Word to
Give the guidance we need,
And we'll avoid the world's pitfalls.
If to it's truths we pay heed.

Take My Life and Use It

I'm sure most Christians want the Lord to use them, and they want to be obedient to His will; and like most of these dear ones, I truly want the Lord to use me and I try to do His will. Although I must admit that at times I feel as though I may rebel a little bit in some way, for I have been transferred many times due to my job, and each time I prayed and asked the Lord to show me His will. I always said, "Lord, I'm willing to do your will". But there were times when I loved where I lived, my friends, my church, and besides any move is hard and disruptive; so, I had to tell the Lord, "Father, I'm willing to move if it's Your will but you know my heart and I really don't want to move." I had to be honest with Him for He knows my heart better than I do.

I have to admit that I have come to the place in my Christian life, that I know for certain, He knows what's best for me and even though my heart tells me one thing and my spirit tells me something else, I can always count on the fact that I'll be happier in the long run letting the Lord lead. There have been times that I've shed quite a few tears, when I had to move away and leave people that I loved dearly, but I knew my Father would show me somewhere down the road, why He wanted me to move. There's a saying, our disappointments our God's divine appointments, and they are always what's best for us. We may not think so today but He will end up showing us the reason.

I have told the Lord, even when I resist His will, I want Him to go ahead and accomplish His will in and through me, whether or not I feel that it's what I want to do or not, for I have complete confidence that He only wants what's best for each one of us. And the only time we'll be completely happy is when we're obedient to our Father.

Read Psalms Chapter 51 and then focus on verse 12-13: Restore to me the joy of Your salvation and grant me a willing spirit to sustain me. Then I will teach transgressors your ways, and sinners will turn back to You.

Read Matthew Chapter 26 and focus on verse 41: The spirit is willing but the body is weak.

Read Psalms Chapter 143 and focus on verse 10: Teach me to do Your will, for You are my God; may Your good Spirit lead me on level ground.

Take My Life and Use It

Take my life and use it, Lord,
In Your own special way,
May it be a blessing used
To brighten someone's day.

Let it count for something that will
Glorify Your name - and
If I hold back in any way
Well, use it just the same.

You have my permission to take
The full...complete control,
(Even against my resistance)
Of body, mind and soul.

I know I have no righteousness
That I can call my own,
And if there's any good in me
It comes from You alone.

Father, those times I may resist
Doing Your will for me,
Please, do what You must to help me...
...Be what you want me to be.

In my heart I know the only
Peace I'll ever find,
Is when I'm completely yielded...
Not just when I'm in a bind.

I know without a doubt the place
Where my joy can be found,
It's in the center of Your will
Where grace and love abound.

The flesh is oh, so weak - but the
Spirit yearns to obey,
So, I ask You, Lord, to take my hand...
And forever lead the way.

It Only Takes a Moment

Friend, have you ever been having a long period of fellowship with the Lord, when things seemed like they just couldn't get any better. Well, sometimes just when we are happiest in our relationship with Father God, the devil must get jealous, for all of a sudden he'll try to knock the props out from under you with no warning. It only takes a moment to interrupt our time with the Lord, and to get us out of fellowship.

Before you know it, you've thought, said or down something that is against God's will, after all in the blink of an eye we can lose our focus and that delights our adversary. But thankfully, it only takes a moment to refocus and then confess our sin and get right back in our right relationship with our Father.

Yes, it's so easy to get out of fellowship but, what a blessing to know it's easier to get back in again. Besides, joy and peace come with getting back in, but a burden of guilt is part of getting and staying out; so, all the more reason to get back in fellowship immediately. All it takes is to confess our sins, for He is faithful and just to forgive us of our sins and to cleanse us from all unrighteousness. I John 1:9.

Once a person accepts Christ as Savior, the next (most) important thing for them to understand and apply, is I John 1:9 for if we don't immediately confess our sins, the Lord doesn't hear our prayers until we do. It says in Psalms 66:18 that if we regard iniquity in our hearts, He will not hear us. So don't wait to confess until just before you pray, instead the moment you sin, confess it to the Lord, or your going to find the longer you wait, the easier it will become, to wait even longer next time. In this race of life, when we fall we must get right back up and start running again. So keep running my friend! Be a winner!

Read II Timothy Chapter 4 and then focus on verses 7-8: I have fought the good fight, I have run a good race, I have kept the faith, henceforth there is laid up for me a crown of righteousness, which the Lord, the Righteous Judge, shall give me on that day but not to me only, but to all them also who love His appearing.

I Peter 5:7-8 Casting all your cares on Him for He cares for you, be sober, be vigilant, for your adversary, the devil, like a roaring lion stalketh about seeking whom He may devour. .

It Only Takes a Moment

It only takes a moment and
Our hearts begin to stray;
Sometimes we may not realize
We've let them turn away.

Just when our walk with Jesus seems
It's really going well;
Satan launches his attack and
He sends it straight from hell.

So child of God you can't forget
To keep your goal in sight
Always looking forward never
To the rear, left or right.

For it only takes a moment
To trip and take a fall;
Each runner in the race of life
Must truly give his all.

If you should start to lag behind
Or even take a spill;
Get right back up and start to run
Or things will go downhill.

But remember as a runner
In this heavenly race;
It really doesn't matter if
You never take first place.

Each time you fall while running
Jesus will pick you up;
Then at the end every runner
Receives a Winner's Cup.

Once you're up in heaven you'll find
There are only winners;
When you're there you'll never hear the
Saints being called sinners.

Tooth Fairies on Strike

Dear Friend, I have included several short stories in this book, in hopes that they'll be a small blessing and that perhaps your children or grandchildren will enjoy them as well. Some, including "Tooth Fairies on Strike" are actually suitable for small children.

Although this is a child's story it has an excellent moral for people of all ages. We are never too old to have (in fact, we should have) the heart and blind faith and trust in the Lord, that a child does. Ask the Lord to meet your needs and often He'll go above and beyond what you asked for, and help others and the Lord will help you. Trust and believe and you'll be amazed.

Read Proverbs Chapter 3 and focus on verses 5-6: Trust in the Lord with all you heart, and lean not unto your own understanding, in all your ways acknowledge Him and He will direct your paths.

Read Psalms Chapter 37 and then focus on verses 4-5 Delight yourself in the Lord, and He will give you the desires of your heart. Commit your way to the Lord; trust in Him and He will do this; He will make your righteousness shine like the dawn, the justice of your cause like the noonday sun.

Tooth Fairies on Strike

Michael was excited, as any four-year-old would be when he lost his first tooth. He remembered when it first started wiggling, his momma said, "Michael, the Tooth Fairy will be coming to look under your pillow." He knew he would have to try very hard to go to sleep and stay asleep. "They won't come unless you are sound asleep," she had told him.

For several days Michael had been twisting the tooth around with his fingers. He was trying hard to get it to come out, but the tooth had been very stubborn. Sometimes after twisting, he would have to spit out a little bit of blood. The tooth had gotten to where it was just hanging by a thread. At last! The tooth finally came out, and Michael, couldn't wait to tell his momma so she could tell him what to do next. He had been anxiously awaiting the opportunity to put it under his pillow. He thought maybe he could go ahead and put it there now, even though it wouldn't be his bedtime for four or five hours. He went running into the living room, where his momma was watching the television, and he was shouting, "Momma, Momma, my tooth came out, my tooth came out. Can we put it under my pillow now?" "We'll get a tissue and wrap it up, and then we can put it in this little tiny box that my earrings came in when Daddy gave them to me for Christmas."

Michael and his mother were totally unaware that behind the scenes the Tooth Fairies' union had gone on strike. There were no Tooth Fairies available to pick up the children's teeth and leave the money. In fact, the Tooth Fairy that was supposed to pick up Michael's tooth and deliver the money felt badly about it, with it being Michael's first lost tooth. But the fairy had to adhere to the union's policies.

Up in heaven, Michael's guardian angel was talking to God about how sad the little boy was going to be, when the Tooth Fairy didn't leave him any money under his pillow. And God said, "I know how sad he would be for I've been listening to his prayers since his momma and daddy taught him how to pray. I've heard all his prayers every night and sometimes in between."

Michael had been praying every night, " Lord, please let my tooth come out and please, don't let it hurt. By the way, I surely would appreciate it if You would please ask the Tooth Fairy to leave me $2.00. I'd like to get that magazine I want with all the pictures of cars and trucks in it. Remember, Lord, I was looking at the pictures when Momma took me to WalMart. If I have anything left, I wouldn't mind if I could get a little matchbox car, but, Lord, as long as I can get that magazine I'll really be happy. Oh, and one more thing, I really hope that You'll give the fairy some good directions, so it won't go to the wrong house. Lord, I've waited a long time for this, and I would be sad if some other kid got my money. But ,oh well, I guess if they needed it more it would be okay but, Lord, I'd still be sad."

So the Lord told Michael's guardian angel, "Let's send one of the cherubs to Michael's house tonight to leave the money so he won't be disappointed. Besides I want to answer his prayer and that will increase his faith. Michael has a heart for Me and He will serve Me when he grows up, and I want to start preparing him for that service now.

That night Michael couldn't wait for supper to be over. He really didn't care about watching T.V., even though his favorite program was on and he did his best to concentrate on it. His mind was on going to bed and getting to sleep as quickly as possible, so the Tooth Fairy wouldn't pass on by because he wasn't asleep. As soon as his program was over, he asked his Momma if she would go into his bedroom with him and tuck him in and listen to him say his prayers.

Michael said his prayers, and his Momma tucked him in, kissed him goodnight and turned out the light. As he lay there, he closed his eyes and tried to go to sleep as fast as he could. He wondered if he wasn't all the way asleep, just almost asleep, but had his eyes closed, would the Tooth Fairy know he wasn't all the way asleep? He hoped the fairy would hurry and come but not before he went to sleep. In a way he wanted to pretend to be asleep, because he wondered what a Tooth Fairy looked like. Would they look like a giant tooth with wings or would it be a little tiny fairy like Tinkerbell in Peter Pan? Soon Michael had fallen sound asleep

At about 2:00 a.m. a little cherub that the Lord sent to make the pick up and delivery, arrived to complete his assigned task. The Lord had told the cherub to take the tooth, and leave the little box under Michael's pillow with $5.00 in it. Michael only asked for $2.00 in his original prayer, and he told the Lord if the Fairy went to the wrong house, and left the money for some other child who needed it more, it would be okay. He said he would be sad but it would be okay. And since Michael was thinking of someone else who might have needed the money, the Lord answered his prayer by giving him more than he asked for.

When Michael woke up the next morning, he opened his eyes and immediately sat up in bed. He then excitedly but hesitantly raised his pillow up and saw the tiny box, and at first thought oh, no, the Fairy didn't come, but he picked up the box and slowly removed the lid. When he saw the five dollars he began yelling for his momma saying, " Momma, Momma, the Tooth Fairy left me five dollars, the Tooth Fairy left me five dollars". His mother came running into the room looking quite shocked and said, "Oh, my goodness, I wonder who could have done that, I guess the Tooth Fairy thinks you're a mighty good boy!"

Michael got up, quickly dressed and went into the kitchen to eat breakfast with his parents. At the table when he excitedly showed his Daddy his crisp new five dollar bill, his father looked quizzically at his mother, and she looked just as puzzled back at him and shrugged her shoulders. When Michael finished eating he couldn't wait to go outside and tell his friends about the visit from the Tooth Fairy. As soon as Michael went out the back door, his mother and father asked each other if they had remembered to leave the money under Michael's pillow. Realizing that neither one of them had remembered to put the money under his pillow, they sat quietly at the table for quite a long time. And although they both felt guilty and ashamed, they felt more dumbfounded and amazed upon finding out neither one of them had left the money. They wondered who might have slipped into the house last night and put the money under their son's pillow.

But Michael knew in his heart who put the money under his pillow, the Tooth Fairy, of course. When the little Cherub who had received the assignment got back to heaven, he told God how excited Michael had been over receiving more than he asked for. The Lord told the cherub, "Men have not for they ask not. And when they ask, they ask with wrong motives. Michael asked for less than he could have, thought of other children who might have needed money, and had the faith that innocent little children have. This is just the beginning for Michael, he is headed for a life of service to Me and our relationship will only get closer."

Michael went to bed that night a very happy little boy. His parents went to bed two very confused adults. The moral of the story is, ask for what you need and you might get more, believe in your heart you'll get what you asked for and come to God with the heart of a child. After all, that's exactly what you really are to God, His child.

Ultimately the Tooth Fairies' union broke the strike. And one Tooth Fairy sent a note to a little cherub in heaven thanking him for substituting for him while the strike was going on. The little cherub wrote back, "Oh, you're welcome. It was all in a day's work!"

The End

The Mask

Dear One, I doubt if there are very many people who live the truth in every way, every minute of every day. Some much more so than others but sadly, most people are a little bit different under certain circumstances. We want the world to see only our best, but there may be times that we say or do things in our home, possibly in front of our family that we wouldn't want the world to see or at least not our church friends . It doesn't mean we're horrible people, for even Paul said, "That which I would I do not and that which I would not I do."

We just need to remember that even if no one else sees or hears us, the Lord always does; and He even knows what we're thinking. We may not   realize it but we can even sin in our thoughts, and if we do we need to immediately confess it just like any other sin. A wrong thought can put us out of fellowship just as fast as a wrong action.

The only thing necessary, to keep us from feeling as though we must wear a mask when we go out each day, is to read and apply (or live) God's Word daily. The Word will keep us from sin and from needing to wear a mask. When the devil tempted Jesus, what did He do? He quoted scriptures, for the Word of God is alive and has the power to protect us and to change a life.

Read Hebrews Chapter 4 and focus on verses 12-13: For the Word of God is living and active. Sharper than any double-edged sword, it penetrates even to dividing soul and spirit, joints and marrow; it judges the thoughts and attitudes of the heart. Nothing in all of creation is hidden from God's sight. Everything is uncovered and laid bare before the eyes of Him to whom we must give account.

And, focus on verse 16: Let us then approach the throne of grace with confidence, so that we may obtain mercy and find grace to help us in our time of need.

The Mask

Before we leave the house each day
We must put on our mask,
People may not know us and might
Be afraid to ask.

It seems as if we live two lives,
One only we can know...
And one we want the world to see
Although it isn't so.

The world sees only our best side
God knows and sees them both,
We act as if there's only one
We'd swear it under oath.

If we would start to live our lives
Like children of the King,
Then when we leave the house each day
Our mask we needn't bring.

We should always take it off and
Then leave it far behind,
Live the same life day and night...
Love others and be kind.

When living life if we apply
God's Holy Word each day,
Then we won't have to wear a mask...
When we go on our way.

When we come out of the darkness,
All things will be just fine,
And we'll be ready when the Savior
Calls, "Let's go, dear child of mine."

The Mirror

Dear Friend, the Word of God is like a mirror, and just as a glass mirror shows us how we look physically, so the Word shows us how we look spiritually. When we look at our reflection in a mirror, if we see that our hair needs combing or we have a shiny nose that could use some powder; we can either ignore what we see, and walk away looking exactly the same way; or we can take steps to improve our appearance. What good does it do to have and look into a mirror if we aren't going to respond to the reflection it reveals and make the necessary improvements?

It's the same way with the Word of God. When we read the Word we are looking into it and we see how we line up to its image (standard). As we read we should allow the Holy Spirit to show us where we fall short and what kind of changes we need to make. Due to our free will, we can respond to the conviction of God's Spirit or we can freely choose to ignore it and walk away in the same condition we were in when we opened the Word and started reading. But what a joy when we read and then apply what we read, for it never fails to improve our spiritual appearance.

Read James Chapter 1 and then focus on verses 22-25: Do not merely listen to the Word, and so deceive yourselves. Do what it says. Anyone who listens to the Word but does not do what it says is like a man who looks at his face in a mirror and, after looking at himself, goes away and immediately forgets what he looks like. But the man who looks intently into the perfect law that gives freedom, and continues to do this, not forgetting what he has heard, but doing it - he will be blessed in what he does.

The Mirror

God's Word is like a special mirror,
Sometimes I look and see;
What oddly appears to be a stranger
Looking back at me.

At times I wonder to myself,
If I'm the only one;
Who's rushed right off to Sunday church
Still looking so undone.

There are days when I look to see
And the mirror lets me know;
Not only is my hair a mess
My face has lost its glow.

Just as that glass reveals to us
The way we really look;
The Word of God reflects our soul
When it's an open book.

It let's us know how we compare
To the truth upon its pages;
A measuring rod that's remained the same
Through all the passing ages.

We often look in a mirror to see
What we should rearrange;
At times we may see all is well,
Or that we need a change.

Look in the mirror of God's Word.
It reveals the real you;
Take action right away to change,
Whatever you might need to.

The Burden-Bearer

Unfortunately, in this world today, there are many people, believers and unbelievers alike, walking through life carrying huge burdens that they don't have to carry. People of all ages, from all walks of life, all races and faiths are allowing themselves to be weighed down with physical, financial, emotional, mental and even spiritual burdens, most to the point of wondering how much more they can take. That's probably a large part of the reason for so many tragic suicides. Their feelings of hopelessness and not knowing how to cope lead them to give up on life. They see no way out.

Those of us who know the way to unburden ourselves, need to be ready at all times to point others in the right direction. Can't you just see them trudging along with their burdens of sin, sorrow, stress and all the cares of the world? They're constantly on the move and yet getting nowhere. What a blessing we can be to these sad, lost, confused people. Think of how they'll feel once they learn to give their burdens to the one and only burden-bearer. The relief it will bring to have such weight taken from their shoulders; setting them free to be all the Lord intended for them to be.

We can point the way to the Savior and He will not only set them free for eternity but He will also set them free from carrying their heavy load day to day. Christ not only saves, but sets free, and yet there are believers that are going to heaven but don't know how to give their burdens to the Lord. They are walking daily with their heavy load just like the unbeliever, and they need to be unburdened as well. God's will and God's way are in His Word and we who are equipped to do so, must direct those who may not know how, to find the way in the Word.

Read Luke Chapter 11 and then focus on verse 46: Jesus replied, "And you experts in the law, woe to you, because you load people down with burdens they can hardly carry, and you yourselves will not lift one finger to help them.

Read Psalms 68:19 Praise be to the Lord, to God our Savior, who daily bears our burdens.

Read Psalms 55:22 Cast your burdens on the Lord and He will sustain you; He will never let the righteous fall.

The Burden-Bearer

Many in this world will travel
Along life's lonely street,
Carrying burdens on their backs
They walk in sheer defeat.

They struggle down the road and try
To smile at passersby,
While in their broken hearts they long
To stop, sit down and cry.

They sometimes feel as though their backs
Are just about to break,
And as they walk they wonder how
Much pressure they can take.

If you don't want to join them in
Their sad lonely travels,
Come and lay your burdens down
Before your life unravels.

As soon as you release them there's
One who will pick them up,
He's the Burden-Bearer, the Man
Who'll quickly fill your cup.

And it will start to overflow
Faster than you might think,
Then from His Living Water you
Can always take a drink

This Gentle One will ever try
To make Himself well known,
Sadly some will still go on and
Carry their load alone.

Jesus is the One who'll take your
Great big bundle of care,
And if you'll let Him have it then
You'll be no worse for wear.

Whenever you feel discouraged
Just call upon His name,
For He's the One who'll take away
The heartache and the pain.

Give the Lord your cares and you'll find
Life will be much better,
He has what it takes to meet your
Needs right to the letter.

The Skinny on Potato Skins

Friend, there are so many people with addictions of different kinds; and this poem is an attempt to help people realize that many things we don't consider to be addictions actually are. Drugs, alcohol, cigarettes, and food are all things that people usually think of when discussing addictive behavior. But there are too many things to mention, that a person can become addicted to; and anything that you cannot control or that has control of you is an addiction. It may not be a thing it may just be a habit of doing something routine and now you can't quit doing it.

It could be a habit of using profanity, over eating ice cream, watching too much television. Anything we do that we can't control has a hold on us and we need to take back control of every area of our lives. Some Christians even use the excuse of reading their Bible, praying or going to Bible Study as their excuse for not keeping their homes up and not cooking for their families regularly. It may be just an excuse but it could also be a form of addiction, for I don't believe the Lord expects us to neglect our responsibility to our family; but instead there should be a balance in our lives. We all need to pray, read the Word and go to church and Bible Study but not to the exclusion of our family's welfare.

What are your addictions? What are the strongholds in your life?

Read II Corinthians Chapter 10 and focus on verses 3-5: For though we live in the world, we do not wage war as the world does. The weapons of our warfare are not carnal, but mighty through God, to the pulling down of strongholds, the casting down of imaginations and every high thing that exalts itself above the knowledge of God in our minds, and bringing into captivity every thought to the obedience of Christ.

The Skinny on Potato Skins

I just love dem potato skins
Oozin' en dat butter,
Wit dat dare bacon an saur cream
Dey gon' be makin' ya shutter.

A'course now dem skins done be
A'make'n duh fokes fat,
But dey goes right on eatin' dem skins cause
Dey don't mines lookin' like dat.

Duh pow'r of dem skins be frightnin'
Fo' when dem peoples be ill,
Dey must'a dun lost der mines
Cause dey eatin' dem skins still.

Den when dey suddenly bees dyin'
Dey wonders what it be,
It bees all duh fat en dem skins
Dose fokes was blind en ne'er did see.

Duh skinny on dem potato skins
Be a' eatin' dem wit care,
Fo' dat debil be dun en dem skins
An he bees givin' yur 'art a scare.

So close dem eyes and pinch dat nose,
An' don't ya be tempted by dat smell.
Fo' when ya be dun died an en duh grave
Ya be smellin' dem skins in hell.

The Skinny on Potato Skins
(Translation)

I just love those potato skins
Oozing in that butter;
With that there bacon and sour cream
There gonna be makin' you shutter!

Of course now those skins are
Makin' the folks fat...
But they go right on eatin' those skins cause
They don't mind lookin' like that.

The power of those skins is frightening
For when the people are ill...
They must have lost their minds,
For they are eating those skins still.

Then when they're suddenly dying
And they wonder what it could be...
It was the fat in all those skins,
But they were blind and never did see.

The skinny on those potato skins...
Be eating them with care,
For that devil is in those skins,
And he'll be giv'n your heart a scare.

So close your eyes and pinch that nose
And don't you be tempted by that smell...
For when you've done died and you're in the grave
You'll be smellin' those skins in hell.

The Soil of the Soul

My Friend, what it takes to cultivate a garden, and then to keep it beautiful and producing to its full potential, can easily be compared to the life of a believer.

Just as a garden needs to be tended properly by tilling, seeding and feeding it; so it is in a believer's life. When a garden has the proper care, it will produce a full, beautiful crop of flowers or vegetables for the gardener to harvest and share with others. Not only will the gardener be able to enjoy it but many others will as well.

When a believer tends the soil of their soul, to do it properly they must read the Word and memorize scriptures, pray and intercede for themselves and others, keep their sins confessed and minister to the needs of others. They need to fellowship with other believers and attend a good Bible-teaching church.

The Word of God is their spiritual food, and it feeds the soil; daily challenges till the soil, and ministering to the needs of others and telling the lost about the Lord, are some of the ways the soil is seeded. Just as a garden can bless many, so a believer whose spiritual life has been nurtured in the right way, can truly be a blessing to many, and they can bring honor and glory to their Father God with the fruit they produce.

Saint of God, take good care of the soil of your soul, till it, feed it and seed it regularly, and you'll be blessed and be a blessing.

Read I Corinthians Chapter 3 and focus on verses 6-9: I planted the seed, Apollos watered it, but God made it grow. So neither he who plants nor he who waters is anything, but only God, who makes things grow. The man who plants and the man who waters have one purpose, and each will be rewarded according to his own labor. For we are God's fellow workers, you are God's field, God's building.

Read Matthew Chapter 13 and focus on verse 8: Still other seed fell on good soil, where it produced a crop—a hundred sixty or thirty times what was sown.

The Soil of the Soul

The Gardner of the Universe
Plants flowers of all kinds,
Such beautiful trees, shrubs and crops
We can't fathom in our minds.

Just the right amount of rain and
Then bright rays from His Sun,
Yields awesome beauty and joy and
Some fun for everyone.

Many crops are harvested like...
Veggies and the flowers,
Filling vases for weeks and those
Growling tummies for hours.

But...to have such magnificence
And results so sublime,
The soil must be tilled and fed
And seeded every time.

First of all the land must be in
A state of perfection,
So ask the great Gardner for His
Personal direction.

My Friend, just like a fine garden
There's the soil of the soul,
And to let God do the tending
Should be our main goal.

We will seldom find our garden
Needing to be weeded,
If we make sure to keep our soil
Constantly fed and seeded.

Read God's Word, pray daily and then
Surrender to His will,
And very soon your crops won't have...
Anymore weeds to kill.

The Thief

The day that Jesus was crucified, two criminals were crucified as well, one on each side; and although they were both thieves they had totally different reactions to their situation that day. One thief was ranting and raving and told Jesus, "Aren't You the Christ? Save yourself and us!" But the other thief admitted his guilt and repented and said, "Jesus is innocent but we're guilty."

In this world, when people are confronted with their sin, they react in different ways. Some people try to deny their guilty, others try to blame someone else for their sin, but there are still those who admit their sin and repent and ask for forgiveness.

The two thieves represent us and the decisions and the choices we make. Even though we sin, we have a choice, when it comes to how we're going to respond to the conviction of the Holy Spirit. Both thieves were guilty and condemned to die but they chose to respond differently. How do you react when the Holy Spirit convicts you; when you're reading your Bible or hearing a message at church or on the radio and you know the Lord is speaking to you? Do you just shrug it off and forget about it, or tell God you did it because someone else did something that made you do it? We can make all the excuses we want to but not one is good enough. For God has given us a way of escape and we never have to sin

When we sin we need to admit and confess it in order to get back in fellowship. But the choice is ours, how will you react my friend? Will you be ranting and raving or repenting and confessing?

Read Luke Chapter 23 and then focus on verse 40-43: But the other criminal rebuked him. "Don't you fear God," he said, "since you are under the same sentence? We are punished justly, for we are getting what our deeds deserve. But this man has done nothing wrong." Then he said, "Jesus, remember me when you come into your kingdom." Jesus answered him, "I tell you the truth, today you will be with me in paradise."

Read I Corinthians Chapter 10 and focus on verse 13: No temptation has seized you except what is common to man. And God is faithful; He will not let you be tempted beyond what you can bear. But when you are tempted, He will also provide a way out so that you can stand up under it.

The Thief

That day there were three crosses
On the top of Calvary's hill;
Two thieves and the Lord Jesus,
It was the Father's will.

One thief hung suspended in space,
There for a reason that he could not deny.
The Man in the Middle committed no crime,
But was nailed to a cross...the thief wondered why.

He heard One Man say, "Father, forgive them".
The other was ranting and raving;
Why'd this man say, "Father, forgive"?
The thief didn't know...the world needed saving.

He deserved to suffer for his crime,
What about the Man in the Middle?
He'd done nothing wrong, so, why'd He have to die?
This must be some strange kind of riddle!

One criminal mocked the Lord...as he hung on the cross,
The other said, "We deserve the punishment given...
But this Man is innocent of any crime...yet,
The crowd seems strangely driven".

The thief said, "Jesus, remember me,
He didn't know God's Son...would die to save the lost.
Jesus said, "Today you'll be with me in paradise,"
The thief had no idea how much paradise cost.

The two thieves who hung beside Jesus,
Represent you and me and the choices we make.
Jesus suffered unjustly for those who should suffer,
But how much should one Man have to take?

Without Jesus' suffering...the world was bound for hell.
But by His death on the cross;
Those who before were lost and hopeless,
They're now no longer hopelessly lost.

Not only would the thief be in paradise that day,
But Jesus' death the world would ever recall;
And those who put their faith in the Savior,
Heaven is now open to them all.

Friend, will you rant and rave over your situation,
Even though it's of your own making?
Or like the thief...put your trust in Jesus,
And find heaven can be yours for the taking?

The Tongue

Friend, the tongue is such a tiny member of our bodies to be so powerful. For its size it is probably the strongest thing in the world. A tiny organ that can, build up, destroy, lift up, let down, it can kill or it can heal, discourage or encourage, spread love or hate, tell and spread the truth or a lie. It can bless or curse and ultimately be used for good or evil.

How will you choose to use your tongue? Will you use it to be a blessing to the Lord and your fellow man or to harm others and to disobey God? The choice is yours!

Read James Chapter 3 and then focus on verses 7-12: All kinds of animals, birds, reptiles and creatures of the sea are being tamed and have been tamed by man, but no man can tame the tongue. It is a restless evil, full of deadly poison. With the tongue we praise our Lord and Father, and with it we curse men, who have been made in God's likeness. Out of the same mouth come praise and cursing. My brothers, this should not be. Can both fresh water and salt-water flow from the same spring? My brothers, can a fig tree bear olives, or a grapevine bear figs? Neither can a salt spring produce fresh water.

Read James Chapter 1 and focus on verse 26: If anyone considers himself religious and yet does not keep a tight rein on his tongue, he deceives himself and his religion is worthless.

Read James Chapter 3 and then focus on verses 3-12: When we put bits into the mouths of horses to make them obey us, we can turn the whole animal. Or take ships as an example. Although they are so large and are driven by strong winds, they are steered by a very small rudder wherever the pilot wants to go. Likewise the tongue is a small part of the body, but it makes great boasts. Consider what a great forest is set on fire by a small spark. The tongue also is a fire, a world of evil among the parts of the body. It corrupts the whole person, sets the whole course of his life on fire, and is itself set on fire by hell.

All kinds of animals, birds, reptiles and creatures of the sea are being tamed and have been tamed by man, but no man can tame the tongue. It is a restless evil, full of deadly poison. With the tongue we praise our Lord and Father, and with it we curse men, who have been made in God's likeness. Out of the same mouth come praise and cursing. My brothers, this should not be. Can both fresh water and salt water flow from the same spring? My brothers, can a fig tree bear olives, or a grapevine bear figs? Neither can a salt spring produce fresh water.

The Tongue

The tongue can be a weapon...or it can be a balm,
It can spew out venom...or it can quote a Psalm.

It can offer up a blessing...or trample with a curse,
It can make things better...or it can make things worse.

Do we use our tongue to malign and condemn,
Or to praise our Savior and to bless all men?

The tongue has the power to kill or to heal,
It can let the world know our salvation is real.

The Bible says, salt water...can't flow from a spring,
Then should mean words come...from the child of a king?

As God's children we should ask ourselves...before we start to
speak,
Is it truly God's glory and the good of others that we seek?

If we use our tongue, the way God wants us to,
We'll sing, pray and praise the Lord and be a blessing too.

We have the free will...to choose this very day...
We can use it for evil...or in the right way.

Before we say a single word...let's get our minds in gear,
Then we can all be a blessing...every day of the year.

The Well in the Desert

Dear One, have you ever felt so alone, that you could be in a crowded room, full of people, and yet you still felt as though no one was around? Perhaps, friends and loved ones have even tried to be an encouragement to you, and yet it seemed as if you were staggering through the desert and there wasn't an oasis to be found. You felt overwhelming sadness and really didn't know why.

I have news for you, Friend, if you'll stop struggling along and searching for something that is already available to you, then you'll be able to find what you've been looking for all along. The only thing that will quench a believer's thirst is Living Water; and it can only be found in one place and that's in Jesus.

Wouldn't it be wonderful if people spent half the time fellowshipping with the Lord in prayer and in Bible Study as they do running here and there trying to find something to make them happy?

Once we are born again, we become a new creation and the new creation cannot be satisfied by the same things, or in the same way. When the scriptures say, "Behold! All things become new!" It definitely means ALL!

Nothing can quench the thirst of the new man but Living Water, and we will never be able to find a substitute for it. Even if we tried all that the world has to offer, we'd still be thirsty. So quit wasting your time and invest it in taking in your unlimited supply of fresh, thirst-quenching Living Water.

Read John Chapter 4 and then focus on verse 10: Jesus answered and said unto her, If thou knewest the gift of God, and who it is that saith to thee, Give me to drink; thou wouldest have asked of him, and he would have given thee living water

Read Jeremiah Chapter 17 and then focus on verse 13: O Lord, the hope of Israel, all that forsake thee shall be ashamed, and they that depart from me shall be written in the earth, because they have forsaken the LORD, the fountain of living waters.

The Well in the Desert

There are times you may feel as though
You are losing your mind.
People offer to help and most
Try their best to be kind.

But even when you find yourself
With people all around,
It feels like you're in the desert
And you can't hear a sound.

You have deep feelings of sadness
And sorrow to the bone.
You're surrounded by a crowd but
You still feel all alone,

Life may seem very barren
And you can't see the light,
At times your thirst overwhelms you
And no water's in sight.

Friend, remember you're a winner,
And the Lord's on your side;
So, when going through a drought there's
No need to run and hide.

Simply rest and don't forget there's
A secure place to dwell,
An oasis in the desert
With its own flowing well.

When your journey hits a dry place
The first thing you should do;
Is drink from your Living Water...
It's there to see you through.

Jesus is that Living Water
We all need to survive;
And if we drink from that well it's
What will keep us alive.

Yes, when we get too weak and fall,
Then He'll pick us up;
And with His refreshing water
He will refill our cup.

My Love My Bill

Several years ago, I went down to WalMart to get my husband Bill a Valentine card, and when I looked over the ones in the husband section, I simply could not find exactly what I wanted. I decided to go home and make my own card to put with his chocolate hearts and goodies. Putting this book together I felt strongly that I wanted to share the contents of the card with you.

I wanted to let people know that a marriage may not be perfect, but if the Lord is the glue that holds it together, it will last through thick and thin. It will last through all the good times and the bad as long as the Lord is the glue that you apply to every little chip or crack. He's the Fixodent for relationships.

One thing I highly recommend is never go to bed angry, always kiss and make up, and say your prayers together before you go to sleep. You can't stay angry if you follow these instructions and it will keep your marriage together. A husband and wife, who pray together, stay together, and that's awesome, but it's even better if you read your Bibles together as well.

Remember, your spouse is a gift from God.

Read Proverbs Chapter 15 and focus on verse 1-2: A gentle answer turns away wrath, but a harsh word stirs up anger. The tongue of the wise commends knowledge, but the mouth of the fool gushes folly.

My Love My Bill

How is it Lord I found a love
That you meant just for me,
I never dreamed that I would find
As dear a love as he.

Looking at my precious Bill - I'm
Thinking as I'm gazing,
Lord your sense of humor really
Seems to be amazing.

You brought two people together
With a quiet dinner,
Bill says he knew right away - at
Last he'd found a winner.

We realized we were so far
Apart in all our ways,
That some thought we'd never make it
For more than thirty days.

We have the glue in common that
Holds it all together,
An anchor keeps it steady in
Clear and stormy weather.

Although I couldn't say that we've
Never had little spats,
And once or twice we've even fought
A bit like dogs and cats.

We always find the time to kiss
And make-up right away,
At night when we turn out the light
We always start to pray.

Valentine's day I'll buy a card
That'll say, "I love you so."
Each year I wonder why for he's
Already bound to know.

Then I stop and remind myself
My FATHER up above.
Blessed me with a special gift that -
I call my Bill - my love.

The Open Book

Some people today still believe we have to get to heaven on our works. Hoping their good works will outweigh their bad works on God's great big scale in the sky. But all mankind should be exceedingly thankful that's not the way it is. If the Lord let us in according to our works, where would the line be drawn, how many and what kind would it take to get in the gates?

From the beginning of time man has proven over and over that he is incapable of obeying God to the degree that it would take to get into heaven. That would take perfection, for no sin can get into heaven. That's the reason why God the Father sent His Son to die in our place. He died to pay for our sins so that we could receive His perfection; His blood covers our sins, and that means when God looks at us He doesn't look on our sin. We are so tremendously blessed to have a Father who loved and continues to love us so very much.

Dear One, if you have never put your faith and trust, in God's Son, the Savior of the world, the Lord Jesus Christ, do it today. Don't put it off for you may not have tomorrow. All you need to do is tell the Lord: Father God, I know I'm a sinner and I can't save myself, and I believe Jesus is your Son and that He died on the cross to pay for my sins. I'm asking Jesus to come into my life right now, to be my Savior and Lord. Help me to be the person You want me to be. Thank You, Jesus, for dying for me, please, help me to live for You. In Jesus Name, Amen

Read Revelation Chapter 21 and then focus on verse 27: Nothing impure will ever enter it, nor will anyone who does what is shameful or deceitful, but only those whose names are written in the Lamb's book of life.

And, Revalation Chapter 20 focus on verses 11-15: And I saw the dead, great and small, standing before the throne, and books were opened. Another book was opened, which is the book of life. The dead were judged according to what they had done as recorded in the books. The sea gave up the dead that were in it, and death and Hades gave up the dead that were in them, and each person was judged according to what he had done. Then death and Hades were thrown into the lake of fire. The lake of fire is the second death. If anyone's name was not found written in the book of life, he was thrown into the lake of fire.

The Open Book

A book's been opened up in heaven,
Many names are written on each line;
As God goes searching through the pages,
I wonder if He'll find mine.

So, I ask myself the question,
"Will He think I did enough?"
But trying to find the answer,
I find is really rough.

For I know there've been times that I...
Could have done some good deeds,
I guess I was more concerned with
My own personal needs.

I did do a few things...here and there
And even tried to show I care:
I'm sure God understands that I...
Had little time to spare.

My life has always been so hectic
And I hope He can see,
There was no time for others and
Very little for me.

I'm sure He makes allowances
When there's too much to do;
He'll weigh my works, good and bad
And maybe I'll make it through.

I guess just now for safety's sake
I'd better ask the question,
Lest I stand before God's throne
And find His court's in session.

What did I hear you say just now,
"Heaven's open to all?
Eternal life's the gift you receive
When on Jesus' name you call?"

It all just seems too simple
But if it's all I have to do,
Dear Lord, You died to save the lost,
Please, won't you save me too?

The Three Wishes

Friend, don't you sometimes wish things could be different in the world? What if you could have three wishes granted; what do you think they would be? It's just something for you to think about.

Would you wish for things just for yourself, for your own pleasure and satisfaction, or would they include good things concerning the welfare of others?

Christians pray for things - we don't make wishes - and hopefully we pray for the needs of others first. Not that there's anything wrong with praying for things for ourselves; but when we intercede for others the Lord seems to take care of our needs even before we voice them. Besides, it's hard to dwell on our problems, when we're concentrating on praying for and ministering to others.

Read I Peter Chapter 4 and focus on verses 7-10: The end of all things is near. Therefore be clear minded and self-controlled so that you can pray. Above all, love each other deeply, because love covers over a multitude of sins. Offer hospitality to one another without grumbling. Each one should use whatever gift he has received to serve others, faithfully administering God's grace in its various forms.

The Three Wishes

Now if I could have three wishes,
The first would have to be;
People learning to love the Lord,
And their blinded eyes to see.

For the second wish I have to say...
The thing that comes to mind,
Is for all men to learn how to
Love others and be kind.

This world would be a better place,
If we would love our brother.
Put the needs of others first,
And each one help another.

For the Lord wants us to help that one
Who might have gone astray.
Show them how to get back home when...
It seems they've lost their way.

If men would give their hearts to God
Then soon they would have peace
For then this world would quickly find
That all its wars had ceased.

And last but not least my third wish
May sound a little strange;
I'd want lots and lots of money,
If God knew I wouldn't change.

I'd use all the cash to help those,
Who fell along the way;
They have no food, no home or love,
They're dreading each new day.

With all my new-found funds I would
Hope to change the world;
First I would erect a cross and then
Our flag would be unfurled

With God all things are possible,
We can truly make them better;
By following all His principles
Right to the very letter.

Feelings and Emotions

Friend, although our feelings and emotions can be so very fragile, still, many people live life according to the up or down mode of their feelings. Sadly, they usually live a very unstable life, due to the fact that they are constantly on a high or a low. Their moods affecting everything they do and their behavior is influenced constantly by their thoughts and feelings.

Some people know that they are extremely emotional, and yet, they're always making decisions according to their emotional state, instead of on fact or when their state of mind is truly sound.

Satan loves to attack the mind of a believer and that is all the more reason why we should not make decisions on any grounds other than whether or not they line up with the Word of God. It's impossible to make sound decisions unless you are in the right frame of mind, and that can only happen when we're being controlled by the Holy Spirit (Walking in the Spirit).

When a person has extreme highs and lows, it is important for them to realize that they need to refrain from making decisions until their mood has leveled off, for if they don't they'll end up regretting it.

If you know you're a worrier, simply remember that worry is a sin and it doesn't come from the Lord. Confess to Him, that you've been worrying and/or doubting, and then lay whatever you've been worrying about at His feet.

My friend, let go and let God!

Read Matthew Chapter 6 and then focus on verses: Be not anxious for the things of tomorrow, for tomorrow will be anxious for the things of itself. Sufficient unto the day is its own evil.

Feelings and Emotions

Don't live life on your changing feelings
But on the unchanging Word of God,
Emotions can lead you down unstable paths
Unfit for God's children to trod.

For it seems they're so unstable,
Just like the wind and the weather;
The Word of God never changes
It's a solid foundation forever.

With our feelings and emotions so fragile...
We all need comfort now and then;
The Lord is the God of all comfort
If you need it, then just tell Him when.

Living life on your changing emotions,
Only brings you sorrow and pain;
And when your 'up' feelings are gone
You're 'down' where you started again.

When you're ready to build your house,
Build it on the Word - the Rock of Ages;
For the Truth of God's Word is eternal
And has Everlasting life between its pages.

The fleeting treasures of this world
Will never meet our need,
But the blessings in God's storehous
Yes, they'll always succeed.

My friend, trust the Lord and His Word - for everything.
Let Him be your All in All,
Once you've found His all-sufficient comfort and grace,
Feelings and emotions can never make you fall.

Favoritism

God is so good, for in His Word, He not only tells us what to do and what not to do, but over and over again He gives us perfect examples of what happened to the saints who didn't listen. Thankfully, it's not all bad news, for He includes His obedient, along with His disobedient, Old and New Testament children. He doesn't stop there; He also includes the results of their actions, both good and bad.

Actually, we are all without excuse, for we have everything we need to live a godly life. And one of the many examples the Lord gives us in His Word, is the results caused by showing favoritism. It may be a parent, a teacher, an employer or a friend, but whoever it is, wherever it takes place and regardless of the reason, it is sin, and totally inappropriate; besides there is no excuse for it. No one in their right mind wants to be slighted by a parent, peer, friend, employer, teacher or anyone else for that matter. It hurts!

If you are being affected by favoritism, don't retaliate, but pray for the one who is sinning against you in that way. Don't let it offend you for it's a sin to be offended, and if you handle the situation in a godly fashion, it can work wonders and heap coals of fire on that other person's head.

Don't worry! Be happy! You're God's Favorite!

Read Genesis Chapter 37 - the entire chapter - but also read the rest of the book of Genesis for it is so wonderful on showing us the foolishness of men and the long-suffering of God.

If you've never read the story of Jacob and Joseph it is a must! It is an awesome example of God turning evil into good. You'll love it!

Read James Chapter 2 and focus on verses 8-9: If you really keep the royal law found in Scripture, "Love your neighbor as yourself, you are doing right. But if you show favoritism, you sin and are convicted by the law as lawbreakers.

Favoritism

Jacob and Rachael were a couple
Who lived long ago,
They had a son named Joseph and
They both loved him so.

Jacob fathered many sons in
Early biblical days,
He loved them all but favored one
In, oh, so many ways.

Rachel had been deeply longing
For some sad, lonely years...
To have Jacobs child and she cried...
Many mournful tears.

Foolishly she told Jacob, not to...
Wait another year more,
But to use the servant, Bilhah."
And soon a son she bore.

Time went on - twelve sons were born but
Rachael bore only two,
And with Jacob favoring Joseph...
Envy began to brew.

Playing favorites stirred up
Jealousy from the ten,
Causing animosity between...
The brothers to begin.

For Joseph - Jacob made a coat - and
Colors - it had many,
But for his other sons - well, he
Didn't give them any.

Jacob's lack of wisdom started
Problems among his sons,
The ten tried to get rid of Joseph
And really thought they'd won.

Alas, they threw him in a well
And thought that he had died,
Then when they told their Father this...
The brothers simply lied.

But God had other plans for the
Boy Joseph as a man,
He'd save Israel from a famine
Before it e'er began.

Things could have been much better
For that whole family,
If only Jacob would have loved
His twelve sons equally.

But the Lord turned evil in to good
And things turned out alright,
But Jacob had ten other sons
Of whom he soon lost sight.

So, to his sons it seemed as if
He really didn't care,
For each one longed to have his love
In their own equal share.

Let's all take the lesson to heart
God teaches in His Word,
To love our children all the same
Just as we've always heard.

Jacob is a perfect example
Of just what not to do,
Don't ever let favoritism
Get it's hold on you.

Yesterday's Gone Now

Why is it that many people try to live in the past? Sometimes it seems as if they are almost afraid to let go of yesterday, for their today may not live up to their dreams and expectations. If only they understood that each day we're given is special and the Lord gives us that day for a reason and a purpose.

Each day is another step toward heaven. My grandmother lived to be ninety-seven and that's a lot of steps, but if she had lived for yesterday she would never have made it. We can learn from the past but we can't go back and change it. Today is a very special day and we need to live it in a way that glorifies God and blesses others.

Tomorrow is another day and there are times that we dread its arriving, and some even get depressed over it before it gets here. Why is it we have a tendency to worry about things that very possibly may never take place? We waste perfectly good time on what could be a great day, worrying about what might never happen.

Friend, let's learn what we can from yesterday and then forget it, use today wisely and don't waste time worrying about tomorrow.

Read Philippians Chapter 3 and then focus on verses 13-14: Brethren, I count not myself to have apprehended: but this one thing I do, forgetting those things which are behind, and reaching forth unto those things which are before, I press toward the mark for the prize of the high calling of God in Christ Jesus.

Read Philippian Chapter 4 and focus on verse 6: Be anxious for nothing, but in everything, by prayer and petition, with thanksgiving, let your requests be made know unto God.

Read Matthew Chapter 6 and then focus on verses 33-34:

But seek first first the kingdom of God and His righteousness, and all these things will be given unto you as well. Therefore, do not worry about tomorrow, for tomorrow will worry about the things of itself. Sufficient unto the day is its own evil.

Yesterday's Gone Now

Yesterday is gone now, and today is a brand new day;
Please, help us learn to let go, Lord, and let You lead the way.

Holding on to yesterday never brings us gladness;
For some who try to live in the past - it brings them only
sadness

And since tomorrow is a day that's out of our hands;
Why waste today concerned about some possible demands?

Fear of what could be tomorrow, or grief from yesterday,
Can only serve to waste the time God gave us for today.

Yes, learn from yesterday, and have high hopes for tomorrow;
But from the past and the future, we should never borrow.

Today is meant to be special; we live it only one time,
Each day's a God-given gift with its own divine design.

All our days are like stepping stones leading up to glory;
Mansions await those who heard, and then believed the story.

We must never let our eyes look back at old yesterday,
For if we look away too long, we just might just go astray.

By looking way ahead, instead of looking at each stone;
One day we may look up and find we're walking all alone.

Let's ask the Lord, to give us...just enough grace for today;
For when each new day comes He'll be there to lead the way.

Who's Watching?

It was back in nineteen hundred seventy-nine when my husband and I and our three children were living in Houston. I was so happy in our new home, and we had wonderful neighbors living on every side. We also had a couples' Bible Study meeting in our home every Tuesday night and the kids were in a great school.

Needless to say I was completely shocked when Bill came home and said: "I sold the business yesterday and bought a larger business in Jacksonville; now we need to go up there over the weekend and look for a house. We also need to put our house here on the market with a realtor, and we probably need to go ahead and do that today."

I sat there with my mouth hanging open. Next I started to cry. My parents and all my wonderful friends lived in Houston, so, I couldn't imagine having to go off and leave them, not to mention, we would be leaving our church that we all loved so much. 'Surely, this man was joking!' Almost immediately, I found out this wasn't a joke.

That weekend we found ourselves on the way to Jacksonville, and after being born and raised in a city of several million people, it was quite a culture shock to arrive in a town of eleven thousand people. There was one tiny Walmart and no really nice restaurants or shopping for twenty-seven miles.

We finally found a house after six weeks of living in the nicer of the two motels in town. I must say I wasn't too thrilled about living seven miles from town and that meant from Walmart, Dairy Queen and the two grocery stores. It was the nicest house we could find in that small town and we really did grow to love East Texas with all its pine trees, hills, ponds and rednecks. Once we got the chickens, cows and horse I really loved it and I - having ended up being the momma to all these animals -didn't mind feeding and taking care of our menagerie one bit. The entire bunch were pets instead of farm animals, and later when we had to move, it broke my heart, I worried for a long time about what happened to each one.

We lived in Jacksonville for three wonderful years and suddenly it seemed as if the world had caved in on us. First the economy in Texas started falling off and we had to sell our business. Many of our biggest customers were closing down and we were losing too much business to stay open and pay all the employees. We declared reorganizational bankruptcy. After selling the business for just enough to pay off our debts we walked away with the clothes on our backs and had to move out of our house and let someone move in and take over the payments. We had been unable to sell the house in Jacksonville and the one in Houston, so there was no equity money to start over. Not too many people were going to East Texas looking for a five bedroom, four and one-half bath home on 10 acres in the middle of an economy crunch.

The Lord had decided we didn't need that big old house on Seven-mile Hill, even if we were having a Bible Study meeting there and I had six little senior citizen ladies that I took to the grocery store and out to eat each week.

It seemed as if the Lord was saying, "You don't need that big house, those vehicles and all that furniture. You need to give three bedrooms, one living room and one dining room of furniture to your pastor and his family, for you're not going to need it in that two bedroom apartment you're moving into shortly. And your son is going to be shot by his best friend - by accident - while they're out hunting. Then your daughter is going to try to commit suicide over an engagement breakup."

Actually the Lord didn't say any of that, but it did happen and on top of it all, our secretary had let everyone's insurance lapse. so when we rushed to the hospital and had our son in surgery, we were informed that our insurance cards showed they were deactivated. We were left with thousands of dollars in medical bills, no money and no insurance.

It was just a few weeks after Debbie tried to commit suicide when we had to move into the apartment and that's where I really learned my lesson.

The Lord was so good to us and when we moved into our new place, we ended up having another Bible Study. This one was with thirty-two teenagers from the apartments, that we would never have met if the Lord hadn't moved us into that very complex. Many of those young people had never been to church and we had such a wonderful time. We didn't miss our house on Seven-Mile Hill at all for the Lord replaced it with something better.

There were two or three different times that we couldn't pay our rent and someone paid it for us, but no one ever told us who it was. God is good all the time! The assistant apartment manager, Jean, was always very rude and sarcastic to me.

When someone paid our rent she said, "I don't know why they did it, since it's just going to be the same thing next month."

As talkative as I had always been, I would avoid Jean whenever I saw her. Bill and I, our daughter, Debbie and her baby, Michael, my son Mark and his friend Jimmy from the Army, we were all living in a two-bedroom unit so it was a little bit crowded, but we were happy, as we went gingerly tripping over each other.

Christmas was coming so I made some goodies and had all the teenagers over from the Bible Study. We were going caroling around the common areas and then back to our place for snacks. The young people had a wonderful time and all the families seemed to really enjoy their singing. We went back in for refreshments, but the kids were more anxious to get their hugs than they were to get the goodies for their tummies. Most of these precious teens seemed to have little demonstrative love, affection and attention at home, for they absolutely craved it when they came over for Bible Study.

The next day our doorbell rang and when I opened the door, a young man with a long beard and wearing a black leather jacket was standing there smiling. He politely introduced himself and we started talking. This nice fellow said," I really just wanted to come by and let you know how great I thought it was that all those teenagers were out on a Saturday night Christmas caroling, when they could have been out getting in trouble. It was so dark last night I don't think you could see me up on my balcony, but I had tears in my eyes when those kids were singing together.

By the way, do you know Jean, the assistant apartment manager? Well, I saw her a couple of nights ago and she was threatening to commit suicide. I'm really worried about her, because she moved here from Dallas to be near her only sister. Jobs are hard to find right now and she was lucky to get this one with our poor economy. It furnished her an apartment as part of her compensation, and now they've fired her and she doesn't know what she's going to do."

We talked a while longer and the young man left. But I couldn't stop thinking about Jean. Since I didn't have the money to buy her a gift, I decided to bake a little tiny vanilla wafer cake and take it to her for a Christmas present. That evening about 8:00 pm., I finished the cake, wrapped it up in foil and put a bow on top. I opened the door and slowly headed out for Jeans's apartment. I dreaded knocking on the door; I was afraid she'd start fussing at me. Me, Me, Me,... it seemed the only thing that mattered to me, was whether or not she would hurt my feelings. I knocked and there was no answer and so I knocked again and still no answer. Whew! Now I can go home and we'll eat the cake ourselves.

Just as I turned around to leave, who was coming around the corner from the parking area? Jean! I meekly held out the cake and said, "Jean, I just wanted to wish you merry Christmas."

I handed her the cake and she thanked me and just fell in my arms crying. We went into her apartment and talked until 2:00 in the morning. We had a very eye-opening and life-changing conversation. I found out Jean's daddy had been a Baptist preacher and he died at ninety years old never having seen his children living for the Lord. I told Jean that her Daddy could see her commitment tonight.

We'd been in our conversation about an hour, when Jean told me that she would see me ministering to all these other people and she never understood why I didn't minister to her.

I said, "Jean, I am so sorry, I thought you didn't like me so I avoided you, and please, forgive me for those actions."

She said, "I saw how you couldn't even pay your rent but you always seemed so happy and you had all those people living in your apartment and everyone else said they never heard you complain. How do you keep from worrying? I'm terrified over losing my apartment."

I told Jean that the Bible says in Psalms 37:, 'Once was I young and now am I old, yet I have not seen the righteous forsaken, nor His seed begging for bread.' So, Jean, that tells me I may not have much but I'll always at least have some bread, and although it may just be a tent I'll have a roof over my head. Regardless of what I have, if I have and you don't have , then I'm going to share what I have with you. And if you get put out of your apartment and have no place to go, you can stay with us, and I'll put Mark and Jimmy on the floor on an air mattress and put you on the long couch. I'm not going to let you be out in the cold.

To make a long story short, Jean prayed to receive Christ that night, went to church with us that Sunday, and that following week the Lord got her a good job and they paid to move her. I reminded Jean, her Daddy didn't see this before he died but he was seeing it from heaven. His prayers were being answered.

I learned my lesson that people who seem the hardest to like or love often need love the most. When Jean told me she saw me helping and ministering to everyone else and she wondered why I didn't minister to her, it broke my heart. But it made me realize that we need to go out of our way to love the unlovely. As the Bible says - feed and clothe our enemies, for we can turn a negative into a positive or an enemy into a friend. We must be willing to humble ourselves and do it, and we'll be blessed. And most of all we never know who's watching what we're doing, for I had no idea that Jean knew so much about me, my family, what I did, where I went and who I was helping. Even if a stranger isn't watching us, our family and friends are. They see nearly every move we make and our choices and decisions may be effecting people and we don't realize it, and in ways that we may never know. Although our actions may affect our children in ways we may later regret, there are times that our actions effect people and result in positive reactions.

My advice to you would be, your actions speak louder than words and since they can have a powerful effect, be aware at all times for you never know who's watching. Treat all men the same and love everyone unconditionally. Be more concerned about the needs of others than you are your own and the Lord will take care of yours.

Beware! You just might be on Candid Camera. God's that is!

Who Is He?

Dear One, have you ever asked yourself the question, Who is this person, the Savior of mankind? Who is He to you and Who do you think He is to the world?

To find out who He really is, first of all, you must have a relationship with Him, by having accepted Him as your personal Lord and Savior. Once you have Him in your life, read the Word daily, to find out what it has to say about Him. You need to know what His Father, the author of the full canon of Scripture, has to say about His Son.

You also need to meditate on Who you truly believe He is in your own personal life. What has He done for you? How has knowing Him changed your life for the better? Has it changed you in any other way?

For me He is not only my Savior, who saved me from an eternity in hell, but saved me from the daily consequences of sin. He's the One who gives me peace in the midst of the storm, calms my anxious heart and He's my protector and provider. He's my very best friend, who will never leave me nor forsake me. Actually, I can't imagine life without Him, for what would be the reason for living? He's all these things and so much more.

In order to truly answer the question "Who is He?" You must have spent time with Him; just as you can't really know people in your church, on your job or in your neighborhood, unless you've spent some quality time together. You might try to guess what kind of person they are, but experiencing who they are is a totally different thing.

If you are unable to answer the question, my friend, please, take time to get to know Him, and start by spending more time with Him.

Read Mark Chapter 8 and focus on verse 27: When Jesus came into the coasts of Caesarea Philippi, he asked his disciples, saying, Whom do men say that I the Son of man am?

Who Is He?

Who is this One called Jesus, the Savior of mankind,
The One who died upon the cross and had us on His mind?

He's the Alpha and Omega, the beginning and the end,
He's the Lily of the Valley and our very dearest Friend.

He's our healer and protector, He's the bright and Morning
Star,
This Shepherd of the sheep, never lets us stray too far.

He's the One who comforts us, when we're feeling blue;
And amidst the storms of life, He'll always see us through.

When all our friends forsake us and we have an empty cup,
He's the One who'll lovingly reach out and fill it up.

He's the first One to forgive when it's mercy that we need;
And when we've lost our way, He'll gladly take the lead.

When all of life's in turmoil and we're in need of peace,
He's the One that we should turn to for His peace will never
cease.

When we let Him fight our battles, He never fails to win,
And if we give our lives to Him, He'll keep us free from sin.

He's the One who died to save us and to keep us all from
harm,
And as His family member, you'll find no cause for alarm.

Please, take time to get to know Him and I'm sure that you will
find,
There's' no other Savior like Him for He's One of a kind.

What is our Motive?

Whatever your gifts and abilities are, when you use them, what is your motive? Do you write, teach, sing or minister to the needs of others, for God's glory and to be a blessing? Or do you do it to try to gain the praise of men, or perhaps just simply to try and make yourself look good? Or could it be that you just enjoy volunteering and being around people?

If our motive is anything other than for God's glory and to be a blessing, we have not only missed the mark, but we missed the point of why the Lord gives us talents and abilities in the first place.

It is such a privilege that the Lord, God Almighty would not only use us in any way, to serve and to glorify Him, but so very humbling that He allows us to be His instruments of blessing to others. We are literally His hands in many instances, when He uses us to minister to people in need.

Read Romans Chapter 13 and then focus on verses 3-13: For by the grace given me I say to every one of you: Do not think of yourself more highly than you ought, but rather think of yourself with sober judgment, in accordance with the measure of faith God has given you. Just as each of us has one body with many members, and these members do not all have the same function, so in Christ we who are many form one body, and each member belongs to all the others. We have different gifts, according to the grace given us. If a man's gift is prophesying, let him use it in proportion to his[b]faith. If it is serving, let him serve; if it is teaching, let him teach; if it is encouraging, let him encourage; if it is contributing to the needs of others, let him give generously; if it is leadership, let him govern diligently; if it is showing mercy, let him do it cheerfully.

Love must be sincere. Hate what is evil; cling to what is good. Be devoted to one another in brotherly love. Honor one another above yourselves. Never be lacking in zeal, but keep your spiritual fervor, serving the Lord. Be joyful in hope, patient in affliction, faithful in prayer. Share with God's people who are in need. Practice hospitality.

What is our Motive?

When we write what is our motive?
To gain the praise of men?
Should it not be to glorify
The Savior once again.

There are those times we sit up late,
Our pen held in our hand;
If only thoughts came pouring out
Available on demand.

But sometimes by God's grace we find...
Words pop into our head,
While we are driving down the street,
Or sound asleep in bed.

God has His ways of giving us
The words we are to write.
Some come in the middle of the day ,
Some in the dead of night.

When writers pen a poem or they...
Choose to write a story,
The words quickly come if they're
Writing for God's glory.

There are times He wants a poem
Written for another,
To lift the sagging spirits of that
Sister or that brother.

We must be ready to listen
To God's Holy Spirit,
But we must be still and quiet
If we are to hear It.

Let's remember when we use our pen
We can make someone's day,
Or leave them feeling sad and blue,
By things we write or say.

Let us use our gifts and talents
Blessing all those we meet,
And for God to get the glory
We must remain discreet.

When You Think You Can't Go On

Dear friend, if you've been going through, what seems like more than your share of troubles and trials, rejoice! First of all if you weren't a child of the King of Kings, the devil would leave you alone, so this is simply another sign of how important you are to the Lord.

When you are going through hard times, always remember, if you'll let Him, the Lord Himself will walk with you through the fire or if need be He'll carry you through those times when you are to weak to make it on your own. When you think you can't go on, simply remind yourself that you've already made it, since it's impossible for you to fail when you are a member of the family of God. You're a winner and all things are possible with Jesus. His Word says, "I can do all things through Christ, which strengthens me."

Know and believe that you can make it, even if it's one step at a time. When you think you can't go on another day, put your hand in the hand of the One Who Can and He will lead you to the other side of whatever circumstance you're going through.

Read I Peter Chapter 5 and focus on verses 7- 10 Cast all your anxiety on him because he cares for you.

Be self-controlled and alert. Your enemy the devil prowls around like a roaring lion looking for someone to devour. Resist him, standing firm in the faith, because you know that your brothers throughout the world are undergoing the same kind of sufferings.

And the God of all grace, who called you to his eternal glory in Christ, after you have suffered a little while, will himself restore you and make you strong, firm and steadfast.

When You Think You Can't Go On

When life doesn't seem worth living
And you're facing sorrow and pain,
Thinking surely this has to be a dream
But you awaken and the pain remains.

You can't go on another minute
And nothing matters any more;
Your heart feels completely broken...
And hope...just left and slammed the door.

It's sad when one of God's children
Feels heartbroken, lonely and blue,
Especially when your loving Father...
Absolutely...thinks the world of you.

Your burden suddenly seems too heavy
For one person to have to bear-
So, go to Jesus and lay it down,
Then turn around...walk away and leave it there.

Be thankful we have a loving Savior
Who's ready to carry our load,
He's there when we call out for help...
As we walk life's long, lonesome road.

Child of God! Get up from that low place
And walk with the Lord as before,
You'll find joy will replace your sadness...
And now there'll be blessings galore.

When you think you can't go on, remember
Circumstances can't get the best of you,
For your heavenly Father will surround you with love
And always be there to see you through.

Be Still and Wait

"Be Still and Wait" is written in what is known as an acrostic poem, and you'll note as you look down the left side of the margin, and read the first letter of the first word of each line, looking down they spell Be Still and Wait on the Lord.

Dear One, this poem is telling you, that the Lord not only has our future under control, but the here and now as well. The Garden of Eden was in a state of perfection until Adam and Eve fell, and even if Eden was perfect, it was merely a foretaste of heaven and all of it's wonders. Nothing we can imagine could measure up to the things God has in store for His children.

We can trust Him with our future and yet many people, worry constantly about everything imaginable, and all for naught, since it doesn't change a thing. And why worry about today when the Lord has it all under control just as He does tomorrow.

We all need to learn to wait on the Lord in complete faith and trusting Him to meet our needs daily; as well as having a peace that passes all understanding, knowing He holds our future in the palm of His hand.

Read Psalms Chapter 27 and focus on verse 14: Wait on the LORD: be of good courage, and he shall strengthen thine heart: wait, I say, on the LORD

Read Isaiah Chapter 40 and then focus on verse 40:31: But they that wait upon the LORD shall renew their strength; they shall mount up with wings as eagles; they shall run, and not be weary; and they shall walk, and not faint.

Be Still and Wait

B etter times are waiting for all of God's children
E den was only a taste of what lies ahead.

S uch love, joy and peace one could never imagine
T here won't ever be a cause for fear or to dread.
I n all of nature, as great as it seems to be
L ittle really can compare with all that awaits;
L ife on this old earth will fade from our memory

A s soon as we arrive at heaven's pearly gates.
N othing this world offers could ever draw us back
D earest loved ones left behind, not fortune or fame.

W hen we get to heaven and see all its glory
A nd hear the Lord God Almighty calling our name.
I n everyday life it's the very same way
T hings don't always happen the way we might plan;

O ur dreams we must leave in the hands of our Savior
N o one can fulfill them like the Son of God can.

T rust Him with all your dreams, your cares and your
heartaches
H e has everything under perfect control;
E ndless blessings are waiting for those who love Him

L et the dear Lord take over and care for your soul.
O nce you surrender, He will be there to guide you
R ejoicing as He sees you coming into view;
D on't fret but be still and wait on the Lord - He waited a long
time for you.

We'll Know the Answer By and By

Friend, so often things in this world happen and there is no way we can possibly figure out the reason why. There are times when our heart has been broken or there has been a tragedy that has taken place in our lives and we in our humanity want to try to figure out why. We want to understand and yet it is impossible.

Even though time passes and we start doing better, we sometimes have moments of weakness, when we start trying to figure out the why once again. Because of His love for us, the Lord wants us to take all our burdens and our cares to Him and leave them there, and yet He understands when we periodically take them back. Sadly, many things that we continue to worry about, we won't know the how or the why until we get to heaven. We would be so much better off if we would as the old hymn says, "Take Your Burden to the Lord and Leave it There", since all the worry and heartache can't change a thing. It only serves to make us sad and discouraged.

Whether it's the stress we're under at our place of employment, loss of a loved one, health problems or problems with a spouse or a child, the Lord wants to take all of our cares from us and relieve us of all our burdens. And although we may find out the reason for some things that happen in our lives, most we'll only find out the purpose when we go home to be with the Lord; and that's why I'm so thankful the Lord gave us the scriptures found below:

Read Proverbs Chapter 3 and then focus on verses 5-6: Trust in the Lord with all your heart and lean not on your own understanding, in all your ways acknowledge Him and He will direct your paths.

Read Psalms Chapter 62 and then focus on verses 5-8: Find rest, O my soul, in God alone; my hope comes from Him. He alone is my rock and my salvation; He is my fortress, I will not be shaken. My salvation and my honor depend on God, He is my mighty rock, my refuge. Trust in Him at all times, O people; pour out your hearts to Him, for God is our refuge.

We'll Know the Answer By and By

Sometimes life is difficult and
We start to wonder why,
Then the Lord reminds us - we'll know
The answer by and by.

He says not to worry but to...
Leave all things in His hands,
Our troubles and our heartaches and...
The world with its demands.

No need fretting over why things
Happen the way they do,
For soon enough the Lord will have
The answers in full view.

Until that time we need to choose
To trust Him in all things,
Although we may not understand
He's still the King of Kings.

When we get to heaven we'll have
Answers to our questions,
But for now we realize His
Commandments aren't suggestions.

We know the Lord understands when
We are hurting badly,
And pain can make it hard to trust,
Still, we'll all try most gladly.

So, for now the things we ponder
We'll just trust and believe;
And then once we get to heaven
At last we will conceive...

For then the truth will be revealed
We'll understand the why,
So, hold on a little longer
We'll know the answer by and by.

What is Your Will?

Dear One, Do you feel like you want to do God's will more than anything in the world and yet you feel like you're His most disobedient child? When you pray you even ask the Lord to help you do His will, and then shortly you're doing your own. And next you're asking the Lord, "Why?"

Don't be discouraged for you wouldn't even be concerned if you didn't love the Lord. You've probably just allowed yourself to get out of fellowship and you can easily get back in simply by confessing your sins. It's called rebound and keep moving. The important thing is do it immediately and don't put it off. The longer you wait the easier it becomes to put it off for longer and longer periods of time.

Don't ever worry about what people think of you just be concerned about what the Lord thinks; for it you're pleasing Him, anyone else that should be aware of your actions will be pleased as well. Also remember the devil's favorite battleground is the mind of the believer and he wants you to feel worthless. Don't! You're not! Surrender your all to Jesus and He will use you in miraculous ways and you will be so blessed.

Read I Peter Chapter 5 and then focus on verses 7-8: Cast all your anxiety on him because he cares for you. Be self-controlled and alert. Your enemy the devil prowls around like a roaring lion looking for someone to devour.

Read Ephesians Chapter 5 and then focus on verse 17: Therefore do not be foolish, but understand what the Lord's will is.

What is Your Will?

I love You, Lord, and want to be
Your most obedient child,
But there are times I feel as if
This child is going wild.

In my prayers I always ask,
"Please, lead me in Your way."
Then turn around and find myself
Unwilling to obey.

Sometimes it's hard to understand
Who I'm supposed to be,
For I'm so busy worrying about
What others think of me.

I need to get down on my knees,
And take the time to pray,
Then read Your Word to see just what
You have for me each day.

Many turn to You...and find that
Your will is in Your Word,
But some continue acting like...
They've never read a word.

But when one of Your children longs to
Walk on holy ground,
You always show that child exactly...
Where that ground is found.

You wrote Your will down in Your Word,
So all the world could know,
And every single word is true,
That's why you told us so.

Your children never need to fear
And wonder what to do,
Your will is in the Bible,
And that will see us through.

From this Moment On

When your whole life seems to be falling apart right before your very eyes; and although you're a believer, you can't feel God's presence in your life like you once did, just remember, that God will never leave you or forsake you. If we don't feel our Father's presence in our lives like we once did, it is never the Lord who turned away from us, we turned away from Him.

The Lord can be pushed down so far on our list of priorities that He has become just a smoldering ember, and yet at one time He was a flaming fire in our lives. He was at the top of our priorities list, and then we started letting unimportant things start coming before Him, and soon they began to crowd Him further and further down the list.

The sad thing is things in our lives will never get better until we fan that smoldering ember back into a flaming fire, until we give the Lord back His rightful place at the top of our list of priorities.

Friend, don't wait another minute, recognize your problem and immediately confess all your known and unknown sins, get back in fellowship with the Lord and this time keep Him at the top of your list and don't let Him slide down even one spot. It's definitely not worth it.

Is it?

Read Hebrews Chapter 12 and then focus on verses 28-29: Therefore, since we are receiving a kingdom that cannot be shaken, let us be thankful, and so worship God acceptably with reverence and awe, for our "God is a consuming fire.

I Thessalonians Chapter 5 and focus on verse 19: Do not put out the Spirit's fire.

From this Moment On

When things around you seem to be falling apart;
It's as though God left and there's a hole in your heart.

You used to feel His presence way down deep inside,
But now there's an emptiness that can't be denied.

What could have happened, He promised He'd never leave;
Written in His Word, but you must choose to believe.

Friend, in times like this we must always remember;
God's a flaming fire...or a smoldering ember.

The choice is ours...

If you can't feel Him beside you, just call out His name,
And soon that burning ember will burst into flame.

Yes, He's always there and He never turns away,
When you can't feel His presence, then you've gone astray.

At times we let circumstances crowd the Lord out;
Then we lose focus and forget what life's about.

It's not the car that we drive and not where we live;
Real joy will only come when our whole life we give.

Yes, when we give our life to Jesus to use as He will,
Instead of a sacrifice we'll find it's a thrill.

From now on when we feel like the Lord's turned away;
When we examine ourselves...then quickly we'll say...

Father, I'm sorry, the problem's always been me;
So, from now on please, help my blinded eyes to see.

I can't make it alone I need You by my side,
And from this moment on won't You, please be my guide.

The mice on the Move

"Mice on the Move" is a short story I decided to write one day when I was reminiscing about a time long ago. We were a young married couple with two small children, and living in an apartment that didn't allow pets. Dogs were forbidden, but cats, birds, mice or fish were allowed.

One day while shopping at the local mall I let my three year old talk me into these two adorable little mice; one was black and white, the other one solid white, and of course both with little, tiny pink ears and noses.

When I look at little mice, puppies or kittens, in fact any small baby animal; it reminds me of how awesome it is to think about the Lord coming up with all these unbelievable creatures. He put them all together, their size, shape, color even their little tiny toenails, ears, noses, every detail, He came up with the idea and then put it into being.

Just think of how many animals there are and they are on top of all the rest of creation, including man, that the Lord imagined, planned and made. How can anyone not believe in God when they look around at man and the world around us?

The mice on the Move

Mary Ann and I had been living in the pet store for several months and no one had been kind enough to buy us and take us home. We had high hopes of going to the same house, and we also had nightmares about being purchased for snake food or worse. There were times we had all overheard customers telling the sales clerk that they needed mice to feed their pet.

Mary Ann and I became closer with each day that passed, so we finally decided to become a real mouse pair. Being a couple made it all the more important that we go to the same home, where hopefully we could start our family and then grow old together, surrounded by our many, many children and grandchildren.

One day I heard a store customer saying she wanted two little mice for pets, preferably one white and the other black or black and white. She wanted them in different colors so she and her husband and their two children could tell them apart.

The minute I heard two in different colors I started hoping and praying the clerk would reach in the cage and select Mary Ann and me; and all the more so since neither one of us heard anything about mice for pet food.

Low and behold, there went Mary Ann and the next thing you know, I felt a hand pulling me out of the cage. The two of us were put in a little box with a few air holes in it and handed to the lady who bought us.

The ride home was so much fun and especially since Mary Ann and I heard the lady pull out her cell phone and call her husband. She chatted for a while and then, She said, "Oh, Honey, I went by the pet shop and picked up two of the cutest little mice for the girls. I thought since the apartment complex doesn't allow dogs or cats, they would enjoy raising these adorable little things."

We started to think we had died and gone to mouse heaven. We were beginning to look forward to getting home and meeting the rest of our family.

We had been living with our new family for a few months when, Surprise! Surprise! The apartment complex started allowing families to have a cat. That very day, our mother came home with a little baby kitten. The family immediately decided to call the kitten Mittens for although she was all different colors - and I believe they said they meant she was something called a Calico - she had four white feet. Since the family didn't know our real names, they decided to call me Marty and Mary Ann became Minnie Lou. I must say it did take some getting used to our new names. Of course our new names were better than being called, Mousy.

I could just hear them calling, "Here, Mousy, here little Mousy."

Our first close encounter with Mittens, took place one night when the girls left our cage door open. Minnie Lou and I decided that after everyone was asleep, we would take a short tour of our home. So about midnight we quietly sneaked out of our cage and started making the rounds. After our adventure had taken us through the living room, dining room and both bedrooms, we stopped by the bathroom for a little dip. The shower had been left dripping and we thought we might as well go for a dip in the largest puddle. We had so much fun splashing and washing each other's back. After our refreshing time in the bathroom we moved on to the kitchen to see if we could find a snack. Sometimes a mouse just likes to have a snack before retiring for the evening.

We had just turned the corner into the kitchen, when we realized Mittens was in there in the dark eating cat food out of her bowl.

Minnie Lou and I thought, "Oh, no! We better get out of here pronto!"

But suddenly we hear Mittens saying; "Please, don't run away, I'd really like to meet you both. My name is Mittens, and I was adopted by the May family about two weeks ago. I've been missing my real family so much, so I hope you'll stay and talk awhile."

I looked at Minnie Lou and said, "Sweetheart, let's stay awhile and talk to the poor thing."

Minnie Lou said, "You know, dear, she does seem awfully lonely. I guess we could stay for a little while."

The three of us had a great time talking about our families and friends and even the adoption process we each one went through. Minnie Lou and I were just saying we needed to get back to our cage so we could go to bed.

When Mittens said, "Why don't you have a snack with me before you go? The food is really not bad at all and it'll be something new for you to try."

We had just eaten a few bites, standing on the side of her bowl, when the light came on in the kitchen and our adopted father saw the three of us eating together.

He hollered, "Honey, come here, hurry! You've got to see this...and bring the camera.

You're not going to believe what I'm seeing!"

Momma May came in and brought the camera and was immediately.....

Exclaiming, "Oh, how adorable! Isn't that the cutest thing you've ever seen, Sweetheart? Be sure and take several pictures since I want one to keep and one to send to the contest in the Enquirer. This is so awesome!"

To make a long story short after picture-taking time we were gently put back in our cage home.

The girls continued leaving our cage open on a regular basis and we finally decided we wanted to move to another location in the house. The next time we got out we found a really nice spot behind the cushions on the couch. It was so nice and quiet and peaceful and so comfy. I gnawed a nice little hole through the outer fabric and pulled out just enough stuffing to make a whole big enough for me and Minnie Lou and the family we were expecting. I carried all the scraps of material and stuffing into the bathroom late that night and since the waste basket in there wasn't as tall as the big trash can in the kitchen, it was easy for me to run up and one mouth-full at a time drop in the scraps.

We would scurry around the house at our leisure and periodically we saw the family and they saw us. We were always faster and smarter, so they never caught us. On many evenings we went and had a snack with Mittens.

One Friday when Father came in from work, after a long hard day at the office, he called Momma May in and asked her to sit down.

He said, "Honey, the company is transferring us to Louisiana and we need to go over and find a house. We can have your mother come over to feed the cat, and we'll leave tomorrow and drive over there and find a motel. We'll stay a week or less depending on when we find a house to rent."

Momma May said, "Okay Sweetheart, I'll get all our things packed and call Mother. Maybe she would like to have the girls stay with her and Daddy while we're gone."

I asked Minnie Lou how she felt about moving to Louisiana, especially with our family on the way.

And she said, "Honey, it'll be a wonderful adventure for us and something to talk about to our children. Besides, as long as we're together we'll be happy and everything will work out just fine."

Two weeks later the movers arrived to take us to our new home; so, Minnie Lou and I snuggled up in our little nest and took our first and last long trip. Of course we didn't get to see much scenery on the way for we were taking our trip riding in the back of a moving van. Although I had to admit it was a special treat that we were able to travel to our new home right in our own home. Mittens was traveling over in the family station wagon, but we were happy going in style as far as mouse transportation was concerned.

When at last we arrived at our final destination we took a tour of our new home on the very first night and although Momma May had not put everything in its place yet, we could still see that we had moved to an unbelievable palace for mice.

It wasn't long before Minnie Lou and I became the proud parents of six babies, three boys and three girls, and over the next year our family continued to grow by leaps and bounds.

Over the years, our family would catch sight of us and finally one night at the dinner table, while they were eating and talking, we heard the news.

Momma May said, "Honey, once in awhile, I catch sight of Marty and Minnie Lou and I think we need to put food out for them. Since we know they're alright let's just let them live wherever they want to in the house. They get along great with Mittens and the girls still love them. In fact, I honestly believe they felt sorry for them living in a cage and they kept leaving the door open on purpose."

Father said, "You're probably right, Sweetheart, and that's fine with me."

So Minnie Lou and I have been living in the lap of luxury and now we're in our twilight years. We've raised all our children and grandchildren and we've been in retirement now for quite a while.

And in closing, all I'd like to say is, "If you're a mouse and you're reading this, always remember, if you don't end up in the belly of a snake, then try to take all your trips in first class. It'll give you and your mate something to talk about for the rest of your lives and even something to share with your children and grandchildren. You can tell them about the time that you were both the mice on the move."

I got it all wrong

Dear Friend, if you know Jesus as your Savior, it doesn't mean you'll never have any regrets, nor does it mean you'll always do everything right. We're not to carry a burden of guilt, but we still know of times, when we've fallen short of the glory of God.

Although there are believers and unbelievers, you'll find that there are also different levels of commitment in the Body of Christ.

There are those Christians that accept Jesus at a very early age, and then never surrender their lives to Him until they are senior citizens. They waste so many years still living as if they didn't know the Lord, but at least they spend the later years of their lives enjoying the blessings that come from a right relationship with Him. The next group consists of the ones who accept Christ and when they die they're going to heaven; they never surrendered to Him while they were on earth and thus they missed out on all the blessings that were available to them.

Too many people spend their lives living as carnal believers and even those who are mature Christians usually have had times in their lives when they haven't walked as close to the Lord as they could and should have.

Personally, I came to know Christ at the age of twenty-five and immediately wished I had been introduced to Him sooner. I was so thrilled and excited about it that I committed my life to Him right then, and I've never regretted it.

I only wish I could say that I have never taken my eyes off the Lord since accepting Him, but there have been times that I have said or done things that later I regretted. I have also let my priorities get out of order for short periods of time and I am so glad my Father God always lets me know it when I need to re-focus.

If you're a Christian, who has put off making a real commitment to Christ, and surrendering your all to Him; please, don't wait another day.

You don't want to realize on your deathbed that you got it all wrong. You never got your priorities straight. Do it now, you'll never regret it!

Read Psalms Chapter 37 and focus on verses 4-6:

Delight yourself in the LORD and he will give you the desires of your heart. Commit your way to the LORD trust in him and he will do this. He will make your righteousness shine like the dawn, the justice of your cause like the noonday sun.

Read Romans Chapter 8 and focus on verse 6: For to be carnally minded is death; but to be spiritually minded is life and peace.

Also read I Corinthians Chapter 3 and focus on verses 1&3:

And I, brethren, could not speak unto you as unto spiritual, but as unto carnal, even as unto babes in Christ.

For ye are yet carnal: for whereas there is among you envying, and strife, and divisions, are ye not carnal, and walk as men?

I got it all wrong

When our mind starts growing dull and
Then our body gives out,
That's the time at last...we seem to grasp...
What life was all about.

Some people don't get it until
Their life is at its end,
And then they find there's nothing else
On which they can depend.

We think to ourselves...if only,
I had known way back when,
What I know today - I'd want to
Start all over again.

People try it all - looking for
A little peace of mind,
They long for joy and happiness
But they're so hard to find.

Wisdom and knowledge are found
In only one single place,
They are hidden to many and
Only found by God's grace.

Joy and happiness are fleeting
And they only abound,
In the center of God's will where...
...His love and mercy are found.

Quit searching all over for all
Those things you think you need,
And the Lord will gladly show you
What you need to succeed.

Let your Father in His wisdom
Lead each step of the way,
Then when your body gives out you
Won't ever need to say...

Lord, I was always so blind and
Why did I wait so long?
I wish I could live life over
Since I got it all wrong.

Blessings for Saints and Sinners

Friend, just think our God is so loving, that the saints and sinners both receive the same opportunity to receive His blessings, which include His unconditional love and His unending mercy. Now, what these individuals do with these blessings and the many others our Father has for us, is strictly up to them. We are free to choose to appropriate each one or to pass them up like they're no big deal. And yet they are not only a big deal, they're the best one we'll ever make or have made available to us. When God the Father sent His son to die for us, it opened heaven up for every person on earth and the only thing that will keep some from spending Eternity there is their rejection of what He's done for us all.

We not only have spiritual blessings but the sinners have the same physical blessings that the saints have; blessings like the sun and the moon and the beauty of nature all around us to freely enjoy, as well as families to be a part of, a roof over their head, employment, and too many others to list here.

The blessings of God cause His children to love and appreciate Him all the more. Hopefully, the sinners will realize what the Lord has done for them and all that He wants to do for them, and will then turn their lives over to Him by accepting Jesus as their Savior. All those who choose to turn their lives over to the Lord will no longer be sinners; but they will immediately become heirs of the King of Kings. At times they may still be sinning- saints but no longer sinners.

Read Galatians Chapter 4 and then focus on verse 7: So you are no longer a slave, but a son; and since you are a son, God made you also an heir.

Read Matthew Chapter 5 and then focus on verse 45: He causes His sun to rise on the evil and the good, and sends rain on the righteous and the unrighteous.

Blessings for Saints and Sinners

Nothing could ever compare with
Love and mercy abundant and free,
They're blessings for saints and sinners,
Freely given to you and me.

You may have all the fame and fortune
This world has to offer to man;
But sadly...that can never bring you
What only the love of God can.

There's no price placed on the blessings,
And there'll be an endless supply,
For you can depend on their source and...
It's one that will never run dry.

Each one priceless...but free to all,
Received by accepting the One;
Who gave His life, and did for us
Things only God's Son could have done.

He offered us eternal life,
And His endless blessings on Earth;
His children start to receive them
At the moment of their new birth.

Nothing can compare to Jesus,
In Him alone are joy and peace,
If you tried to record His blessings
You'd find, that list would never cease.

Why not accept Him as Savior?
If you do it without delay;
You'll find that your many blessings,
Will be starting this very day!

How Can We Not Believe?

Dear One, have you ever thought about all the things that our wonderful God has done for us? If there is anything wrong with this world we live in, it is certainly not our Father's fault. All the things we can find wrong with our planet have been caused by man, not by the Lord.

When you consider the world and the universe and all that it consists of, and how everything holds together and functions so perfectly; there's no way a person with a sound mind can't know that there has to be a God. Think about how a baby is conceived and so intricately forms in the womb and then once it's born, the way it continues to grow into a functioning adult human being.

Think about the beauty of nature and all the many species of animals, fish, birds and even insects, the whole thing is simply awesome. To think our Father made it all just for us to enjoy and we not only take it for granted but there are many who use and abuse it. I'm not talking about by drilling for oil, it's the careless way we live and throw trash every where, abuse one another and even the animals.

Only a God with a love beyond measure, beyond comprehension could create such a fantastic environment for His children to live in; and then to be so longsuffering with us after watching us be so thoughtless and unappreciative.

How can anyone not believe?

Read Romans chapter 1 - be sure to read it all and then focus on verses 18-20: The wrath of God is being revealed from heaven against all the godlessness and wickedness of men who suppress the truth by their wickedness, since what may be known about God is plain to them, because God has made it plain to them. For since the creation of the world God's invisible qualities—his eternal power and divine nature —have been clearly seen, being understood from what has been made, so that men are without excuse.

How Can We Not Believe?

There's the sun, and the moon and the stars in the sky,
The sparkle and the twinkle in a baby's eye,

We can sail the rivers and oceans - even the deep blue seas,
Enjoy the pretty flowers and the tall stately trees.

We can stroll through the valley or climb the highest hill,
Hear the song of the robin perched on our windowsill.

When it storms we see the lightning and hear the thunder roar,
We can see the ships at sea as we stand upon the shore.

Then there's the big old elephant with his funny trunk;
And a stinky little critter...that we all call a skunk.

The list would last forever if we were naming everything...
That we all receive...from our Father, Savior and King.

So, we must ask ourselves the question, "How can we not
believe?"
When as one of God's children all these blessings we receive.

But more than all of the blessings this old world can hold,
More than fortune or fame - more than silver or gold,

It's having the presence of the Lord in our lives
That makes life worth living until our last day arrives.

Do I Want to Die?

I am so thankful that I was never a smoker, although both my parents were, until they were in their fifties and had accepted Christ as their Savior. Even my husband was a smoker for years. I can't say I never tried a single cigarette for I did; and I wish I had a wonderful story of how the Lord delivered me from their hold, but that's not how it was. I tried them for a short period, and just decided one day, that I didn't like the way I looked with a cigarette in my hand or mouth, so I threw them away. I can honestly say I never needed or wanted another one. I accepted Jesus as my Savior when I was twenty-five and had quit several years before, so I can't say the Holy Spirit convicted me and the Lord delivered me.

We all have strongholds in our lives and we need the Lord's strength and wisdom to be set free. His wisdom is found in His Word, but it is up to us to pick it up, take it in and apply its principals.

I judge no one for smoking, but I must say I found out at thirty-five I was highly allergic to the tobacco plant and that was why I had so many respiratory problems growing up (for I lived in a home with both parents smoking) but they didn't know the far-reaching consequences to that habit back then. It's a wonder I didn't kill myself when I tried it. It didn't help that my husband smoked for a number of years, and even though he always smoked outside, the residue from the tobacco plant was still on his clothes and in his hair. To survive I took allergy shots every week until he quit.

I wrote the poem "Do I Want to Die" for a friend who desperately wanted to quit and eventually did. The poem was my way of encouraging her to stick to it. I know so many people try to quit for years and yet like my momma and daddy, they couldn't quit permanently until the Lord delivered them. Remember... I can do all things through Christ which strengthens me.

Read II Corinthians Chapter 10 and then focus on verses 4-6: For the weapons of our warfare are not carnal, but mighty through God to the pulling down of strong holds; casting down imaginations, and every high thing that exalteth itself against the knowledge of God, and bringing into captivity every thought to the obedience of Christ; And having in a readiness to revenge all disobedience, when your obedience is fulfilled.

Do I Want to Die?

I started young and it's so hard...
They'll be the death of me;
I'm in their grasp - they won't let go,
They have a hold, you see.

I remember Momma saying
Start and you will ne'er stop;
But put them down and walk away
And you'll come out on top.

She said they'd turn my teeth yellow,
And cause my breath to smell;
Lungs would be turned black as soot,
By the cancer stick from hell.

Sadly cigarettes cause me to...
Use them as a filler;
When I'm bored I need them even
If they are a killer.

Now that I can't let go of them,
They leave my fingers stained,
Even with a manicure
I sometimes feel ashamed.

I must find something else to hold,
Within my empty hand;
And close my ears completely when
The cigs' make their demand.

Lord, I pray that You will give Your
Divine strength to me,
So, when tempted I'll remember
That You have set me free

Now I'm so glad I asked myself,
"Do you want to die?"
That made me drop those cancer sticks,
In the twinkling of an eye.

Do I Know You?

Dear One, when you get to heaven wouldn't it be shocking if the Lord, saw you at the gates and asked the question, "Do I Know You?" And it was due to the fact that He heard from you so seldom, and had so little real quality communication with you, He didn't recognize you as one of His children.

Would we actually recognize or remember a person we saw very seldom and possibly only every few weeks, months or even years? We keep our relationship fresh with the Lord by praying (our talking to the Father), reading His Word, going to church and hearing the Word (Letting the Lord talk to us and our listening to what He has to say).

Is that what we would want to hear? Even though we would still get into heaven, it would be so embarrassing and humiliating to hear our wonderful Father God say that, after all He's done for us.

Although many will be in heaven, who never gave the Lord any time or attention after accepting His free gift of salvation, but they'll have no rewards and nothing to cast at Jesus' feet.

Will you have any crowns to lay at the Savior's feet?

Do you have your priorities in order, so that you'll never have to hear God say, "Do I Know You?"

Read I Peter Chapter 5 and then focus on verse 4: And when the Chief Shepherd appears, you will receive the crown of glory that will never fade away.

Read I Corinthians Chapter 9 and then focus on verse 25: Everyone who competes in the games goes into strict training. They do it to get a crown that will not last; but we do it to get a crown that will last forever.

Read II Timothy Chapter 4 and then focus on verses 7-8: I have fought the good fight, I have finished the race, I have kept the faith. Now there is in store for me the crown of righteousness, which the Lord, the righteous Judge, will award to me on that day—and not only to me, but also to all who have longed for his appearing

Do I Know You?

When we die and go to heaven,
What will we hear that day?
I hope not, "Do I know you?" but
What will our Father say?

Will He recognize us - from our
Sweet times spent in prayer,
Or have we been forgotten since
Those times with Him were rare.

I long to hear my Father's words,
And I hope they will be,
"My child, I am so glad at last,
That you've come home to Me."

There will be those who'll hear God say,
"My friend, do I know you?"
For they accepted Jesus but...
That's all that they would do.

Rewards to cast before the Lord...
This bunch won't have a one,
On earth they had no time for God
They had to have their fun.

Yes, they got into heaven...but
Their bank of rewards broke,
And they came so close to hell that...
They still smell just like smoke.

Sadly, others will hear the words,
"I never knew your name."
For when they were alive on earth
To them life was a game.

Some will weep and others mourn when
They hear the Savior say,
"I called but you didn't answer-
Too late to come this way."

They could have been in heaven by...
Our God's amazing grace.
Instead they'll spend eternity
In a terrible place,

Yes, God loves us - but we must make...
A choice with our free will,
And for all those who choose the world
For hell they'll pay the bill.

While you're living on this earth, please...
Choose the right way, my friend,
So, you won't have to hear the words...
"Do I know you?" in the end.

A Lion Named King

"A Lion Named King", is a short story that I included in this book in hopes that you'll not only enjoy it but read it to your children so they can enjoy it as well. The story is a picture of what seems like an ideal life style, just as an unbelieving home like I was brought up in; and the Lord in His own way rescuing us from that environment. I was raised in a very happy, moral home but we only went to church once or twice a year (Easter was one of the times that we always went). We never even realized we didn't know the Lord. Once I got saved, eventually my parents and my brother and his wife and numerous neighbors and friends found Christ as well.

Just as many individuals go through some difficult trials before they find the Lord, and that is often what directs them to Him, in this story King goes through some hard circumstances but, just as the Lord brought Joseph out of dire circumstances into his high position in Egypt in order to save His people from the famine, King ends up in a wonderful life in the movies and in a beautiful retirement home for animals.

The story also reminds us that the Lord wants us to take care of our animals.

Read Matthew Chapter 10 and then focus on verse 29: Are not two sparrows sold for a farthing? and one of them shall not fall on the ground without your Father knowing it.

Read Genesis Chapter 50 and focus on verses 39-21: And Joseph said unto them, Fear not: for am I in the place of God? But as for you, ye thought evil against me; but God meant it unto good, to bring to pass, as it is this day, to save much people alive. Now therefore fear ye not: I will nourish you, and your little ones. And he comforted them, and spake kindly unto them.

The Lord can take dire circumstances and turn them into a blessing. Trust Him through your trials until they pass by and then see the joy come that He has in store for you.

A Lion Named King

Hi, friends! My name is King and I'm a retired lion. I happen to be living at this beautiful retirement community for old circus and movie animals and others that have been rescued from abusive situations. Many years ago, before the movie people caught me and brought me to live in America, I lived in the jungle with my family.

I was just a four-month-old cub when they took me away from my home and my people; I was so afraid. Even though things weren't always perfect when I lived at home, at least our family was still together. I have to admit that sometimes life was hard, for we had to wait on our food, and it wasn't always there right when we got hungry. We usually had to wait for Momma or Daddy to bring it to us, and sometimes that took quite a while. Why, even the water was sometimes in short supply, so when we would come across a puddle or a stream we'd all quaff it down like crazy.

There was this one time, just after I was born, that we all had to run for our lives because someone had set a fire in the jungle and Momma and Daddy led us to safety. I was really scared when that happened but little did I know what was going to happen next. I never dreamed that in a few months I would be trapped and taken to live in a faraway land; and that I would never see my family again.

At first I really missed Momma, Daddy and my two sisters, Amber and Indigo, in fact I cried and cried for a long time. I thought about my family so much that I even told God that if He'd let me go home I'd never make fun of Indigo again. I always knew Amber was a nice name for a golden lion for that's the color of our hair, but Indigo? Well, it was only natural for a brother to make a little joke out of something like that. But you have to admit it's kinda funny, when you think about a lion with blue hair. I always wondered why my parents named my sister Indigo when she didn't even have blue eyes, much less hair.

Of course I like the color blue, but there were times when I looked at Indigo, that I couldn't help but picture her with blue hair. And then I'd start kidding around. I'd say things like, "Indigo don't be blue, I wish I had blue hair just like you. I'll bet you wish you had blue eyes too!"

Naturally, I was just joking and after all I thought I was pretty good at coming up with all those words that rhymed. For some reason my sister never seemed to think my jokes were very good, but really, I didn't mean to hurt her feelings, I was just being a cub.

When I first arrived in America I was so afraid for I really didn't understand what was going on or what was happening to me.

Although I was taken in by a wonderful family for my training in preparation for my future, I must say I still grieved over being separated from my loved ones. I thought about them constantly at first, and I would cry myself to sleep at night. You must remember I was just a youngster when I was taken away and I wanted my momma and daddy for the longest time. All I could do was pray that the whole family was okay.

After I started getting a little older I began to realize that maybe I couldn't be with my family, but I could be worse off. Instead I had it pretty good for a lion. After all, when I lived in the jungle things could be pretty rough.

Funny, but I was used to telling my parents and my sisters that someday I was going to be something special, not just any old lion, but they would all just scoff at me and laugh.

They'd say in chorus, "Oh, sure you are King! King's going to be special! Yeah, right! Sure you are!"

After being so afraid, when I first arrived in America, I started to think about how good God was to me. After all He doesn't just love people, He loves lions too. The people that trained me for my movie roles, loved me and treated me like a member of the family. Things were so good at home that I constantly found myself unconsciously starting to purr.(You know people don't think lions purr - but we do under certain circumstances) I was tremendously blessed to spend so many wonderful years with those great people. Many of the other animals that were brought to America for the movie or circus life weren't treated nearly as well as I was.

After all those years working in movies and plays, at last my retirement had come. I paid my dues as they say and so it was time for me to be able to relax a little. Now I'm living in this fabulous place with all this beautiful scenery and three great meals a day. If I get hungry in between meals you're liable to catch me eating mangos and other fresh fruits over there under that coconut tree. In fact my only complaint about this place is that it's a little too close to the freeway and I can hear all the vehicles when they honk their horns. But then I guess a retired lion can't have everything.

I didn't realize how blessed I've been until I heard the many sad stories from some of the other residents here. The ones who were rescued have certainly told me some very heartbreaking tales.

By the way, if you're ever out here in Hollywood, drop by and see me at the Old Animals Home for the Retired and Rescued on Santa Monica Blvd. We can have all the time together we want and I can tell you all about my career. I only regret my family never knew that I did turn out to be special after all, but I'll tell them all about it when I see them in animal heaven.

But they probably won't believe me and they'll just say, "Sure, King, sure you were! Yeah, right!"

I Stand Amazed

"I Stand Amazed" was written as a verse to be sung to the tune of "Amazing Grace" and it can also be read as a poem. The words were written to remind us of not only what the Lord has done for us, but to encourage us to ask ourselves the question, "Would I be willing to die for someone else's good?" We need to remember that Satan would be attacking us with every reason why we shouldn't do it. He'd probably be whispering in our ear saying, "Why go through this for someone who doesn't deserve it?" or perhaps, "The Lord wouldn't want you to do this, you just think that's what He's telling you to do."

Child of God, remember, the Lord may never call us to die for anyone else but are we surrendered to Him and willing to do His will in all things? Whatever He calls us to do He will give us the strength to do it.

We must also never forget that He is with us in the sunshine and the rain, the great times and the very difficult times, at all times our Savior is with us.

Read John Chapter 15 and then focus on verse 13: Greater love hath no man than this; that a man lay down his life for his friends

Read Matthew Chapter 4 and be sure to read it all and focus on verses 1-11:

Then Jesus was led by the Spirit into the desert to be tempted by the devil. After fasting forty days and forty nights, he was hungry. The tempter came to him and said, "If you are the Son of God, tell these stones to become bread."

Jesus answered, "It is written: 'Man does not live on bread alone, but on every word that comes from the mouth of God.'"

Then the devil took him to the holy city and had him stand on the highest point of the temple. "If you are the Son of God," he said, "throw yourself down. For it is written: "'He will command his angels concerning you, and they will lift you up in their hands, so that you will not strike your foot against a stone.'"

Jesus answered him, "It is also written: 'Do not put the Lord your God to the test."

Again, the devil took him to a very high mountain and showed him all the kingdoms of the world and their splendor. "All this I will give you," he said, "if you will bow down and worship me." Jesus said to him, "Away from me, Satan! For it is written: 'Worship the Lord your God, and serve him only." Then the devil left him, and angels came and attended him.

I Stand Amazed

I stand amazed a King would come
To die on Calv'ry's tree,
And all because of love He came
To save the likes of me.

Should I be called to give my life
For others in this world,
I pray that I'll be willing, Lord,
Though Satan's darts are hurled.

And should I fear what lies ahead
Please, lead me night and day,
In sunshine and in raging storms
Be with me all the way.

Help me to trust You, Lord, when times
May get so hard to bear,
And never let me e'er forget
That you are always there.

You told me in Your Holy Word,
Leave burdens at Your feet,
I'm looking forward to the time
When face to face we'll meet.

I stand amazed a King would come
To die on Calv'ry's tree,
And all because of love He came
To save the likes of me.

In the Twinkling of an Eye

Dear One, my prayer for you is that you know the Lord Jesus Christ in a personal, saving way, for you never know when Father God is going to send His Son back to pick us up. The day that time arrives, all those who are unprepared for His return will be left. This very special day, set aside for those who know Christ as their Savior, is called the Rapture.

When Jesus steps out of the clouds to call His children home, it will all take place in a moment, in the twinkling of an eye, and we will all be gone. The dead in Christ will rise up from the grave first and then those who are alive will be caught up together with them to meet the Lord in the air. Oh, what a day that will be and just remember this could be the day.

We should all want to be living for the Lord when He comes, and until He does, we need to be telling everyone we meet that He's coming soon. It should be our priority to tell others how to be ready for that day.

The minute we're all gone, the time of the Tribulation starts and it will last for seven years. We don't want anyone we know and love, not even a stranger who crosses our path to go through that terrible time if we can keep them from it. Simply make it your goal to tell everyone how to be ready for the trumpet's sound.

Read I Thessalonians Chapter 4 and then focus on verses 16-18: And the Lord Himself shall descend from heaven with a shout, with the voice of the archangel, and the trumpet call of God, and the dead in Christ shall rise first. Then those who are alive and remain, shall be caught up together with them to meet the Lord in the air. And so shall we ever be with the Lord. Wherefore comfort one another with these words.

Be ready for this could be the day!

In the Twinkling of an Eye

The Lord said soon He's coming back
To take us home to stay,
And Friend, you never know for this
Could be that very day.

Will you hear old Gabriel's trumpet...
When he blows his mighty horn?
Or will your ears be deaf on that
Great resurrection morn?

When Jesus comes to take us to
Our home beyond the sky,
It will happen in a moment -
The twinkling of an eye.

Our feet will suddenly lift off
Right from this earthly ground,
With the angels leading the way
We'll all be homeward bound.

We'll head out for the grandest place
Our eyes have ever seen,
Where the sky is always blue and
The grass is always green.

All the saints will have a mansion
We'll live forevermore,
With the Lord, our friends and angels
And those who've gone before.

So, we all need to be ready
When Jesus comes to call,
He'll take us home to glory
Where we'll all have a ball.

Remember that He is coming
As a thief in the night,
And when you least expect it you
Will find Him just in sight.

The day our Father calls there'll be
No time to say goodbye,
So...
Have your house in order and let's
All be ready to fly.

Murder

Believer, the Word of God has much to say about the tongue, for the tongue is a small part of the body, but for its size it's the most powerful. When we allow the Lord to use (control) our tongue, it can bring life to one that is spiritually or emotionally dead. It can build up, encourage, bless, strengthen the one who is weak or lift the spirit of the downhearted.

The tongue can be used to do so much good but it can also be used to do tremendous evil. Cruel words from anyone, but especially someone we love, can pierce as deeply or deeper than a dagger. I honestly believe it has caused physical illness or even death due to stress, and sometimes even suicide due to severe depression. And yet no one goes to prison for a deadly tongue.

Some Christians don't even make an effort to control their tongue. Like the old saying, if it feels good do it; apparently it makes them feel big, superior, in control or important to say whatever they please to people. They get high on hurting others; but I believe it's actually a sickness and a total lack of self-control. Self-control is one of the fruits of the Spirit and one guaranteed way of having it is to walk in the Spirit.

The Word of God says the tongue is an unruly evil that no man can tame. But we can give the Lord control of our tongue and then it will be used for good and as a blessing.

Read Proverbs Chapter 15 and focus on verses 1-4: A gentle answer turns away wrath, but a harsh word stirs up anger. The tongue of the wise commends knowledge, but the mouth of the fool gushes folly.

The eyes of the Lord are everywhere, keeping watch on the wicked and the good. 4 The tongue that brings healing is a tree of life, but a deceitful tongue crushes the spirit.

Murder

First mistake, you lost your temper,
And then picked up the knife;
It took but a single moment...
To snuff out the man's life.

The world's label, a murderer,
It's life without parole;
There are two broken families
Whose hearts will ne'er be whole.

Yes, it is true - you did the crime,
That you did not deny;
But what about the ones in court
Who hoped that you would die?

The Bible says that we can kill
Without a knife or gun;
Our words cutting and piercing -
The weapon we use - our tongue.

The words that we may choose to say,
And how they are spoken;
Can destroy a life, crush a soul,
Or leave a heart broken.

When we all stand before the Lord,
What will we hear that day,
"A knife, a gun - perhaps the tongue,
It's murder either way."

My friend, are you a murderer?
Put your weapon away;
Or if you must bite off your tongue,
But, please, do not delay.

You may not have used a gun or knife,
But know that assuredly;
With your words you've pierced a heart
And thought no one could see.

The Lord heard each word that you used
To break that heart in two;
So, judge not the one who used a gun
You're a murderer too.

The Laughing Button

Friend, I don't know about you but if I've been feeling a little bit down, I know it makes me feel so much better when I can watch a good, clean, funny movie. It's almost magical, but I know the Lord had to have given us the ability to laugh for a reason. They say laughter makes you live longer, although on that subject, I believe our days were numbered before we were born.

When my precious Grandmother, MeMe, went home to be with the Lord, and again when Daddy went to heaven; right after their funerals, I took my Momma and the children and grandchildren to a great comedy that happened to be playing at a local movie theater, and the laughter did us so much good. Truly the Lord blessed us when He gave us the gift of laughter.

It's amazing what a little giggling can do! There is no other purpose for laughter other than to make us feel happy. It can lift your spirits when you're down and help you have a better day when things aren't going well. What a blessing, that our Father thought of absolutely everything we would need to make it through this world. He wanted things to be as pleasant as possible; we're the ones who sometimes forget to take advantage of all that we have available to us.

Read Psalms Chapter 2 and then focus on verse 4: The One enthroned in heaven laughs; the Lord scoffs at them

And Psalms Chapter 59 and then focus on verse 8: But you, O LORD, laugh at them; you scoff at all those nations

The Laughing Button

My Father gave me a laughing button,
To use when I feel glad;
But I can also press that button - when I'm...
Feeling lonely and sad.

Yes, He knew laughter - would play a...
Very important role;
Since it's a great medicine - for those who're...
Sick in body and soul.

It's something greatly needed by
Saints who are sick at heart;
And each time you press that button - you'll find...
Joy gets a brand new start.

You can't stay downhearted when...
You're walking on a cloud;
Instead of being discouraged - soon...
You'll be laughing out loud.

Been feeling sick and out of sorts?
Tap your button one time.
And if you can't find yours - then I'll...
Most gladly loan you mine.

So, don't waste a single minute,
Feeling lonely and blue;
Keep your laughing button handy - for God...
Wants you to use it too.

He wants all His children happy,
Shouting from the mountain top;
So, even when we get to heaven - the laughter...
Still won't come to a stop.

Thank You, Lord

Dear One, please, one of these days, take the time to make a list of your wonderful blessings, and then take as long as you need to, in order to truly thank your Father God and show Him your real appreciation for His unconditional love and His awesome provisions He has made for all of His family members.

We have so many undeserved privileges and we should ever be mindful and thankful for them all. Besides, don't you love it, when someone you love thanks you for something you've done, and they do it in a very sincere and loving manner. It makes you feel so happy and I'm sure the Lord loves to know that we love and appreciate Him.

And another thing is, you can't over do it or do it too frequently, in fact it's probably never quite enough.

Read Psalms Chapter 136 and then focus on verse 1: Give thanks to the Lord, for he is good, His mercy endures forever.

Read I Corinthians Chapter 5 and focus on verse 16-18: Be joyful always; pray continually; give thanks in all circumstances, for this is God's will for you in Christ Jesus.

Read II Corinthians Chapter 9 and then focus on verse 15: Thanks be unto God for His indescribable gift.

Thank You, Lord

How can I say thank You, Lord
For all You've done for me?
Blessings that some times...sadly,
I simply could not see.

I thank You for my family
And their undying love,
Those living here on earth...and those...
Living in heaven above.

I want to thank You for my friends,
Each a unique blessing;
They keep me on my toes and some
Even keep me guessing...

...Since I often wonder why...I've,
Been given in such measure;
The joy of my friends and each one's...
A special treasure.

Thanks for letting me live in the...
Home of the brave - land of the free,
And there's no other place on Earth
That I would rather be.

Thank You for the many blessings
You give to me each day,
Allowing me to help someone...
Who might have lost their way.

Occasions when You healed my body
Or numbed my aches and pains.
The many times You took my losses
And turned them into gains.

You sent me my own angel to...
Guard me along my path,
To protect me from the devil's darts...
And from his demons' wrath.

Then when my heart's been broken
You've made it just like new,
And my joy has been restored by
My One and only You.

Lord,

I love You so very much, but I
Could never - even in praise,
Truly describe the way I feel
And will for all of my days

My list could truly go on and on
And I wish the world could see,
For I want to shout when I think about,
All that You've done for me.

The Woman at the Well

Friend, John the disciple in the book of John chapter four lets us know that opposition is already rising against Jesus from the Pharisees. They had become resentful of His popularity and His message as well, for it challenged much of what they had been teaching.

Jacob's old well was located on the property originally owned by Jacob; it was not spring-fed but rain water and dew seeped into it. The Samaritan woman, probably came to the well at an odd time of day, for she knew the other women came in the morning and evening and she was there at noon, and more than likely trying to avoid the other women who knew her reputation. Jesus gave her a message about pure and fresh water that would quench her thirst forever.

Being a Samaritan meant this woman was a member of the hated mixed race, and she was known to be living in sin. No respectable Jewish man would talk to a woman under such circumstances. But Jesus started a conversation with her, for He said the gospel is for every person, no matter what his or her race, social position or past sins. We must all be prepared to share the gospel any time or any place; and to be willing to cross all barriers, and all who follow Him should be willing to do no less.

Read John Chapter 4 and then focus on verses 7-22: When a Samaritan woman came to draw water, Jesus said to her, "Will you give me a drink?" (His disciples had gone into the town to buy food.)

The Samaritan woman said to him, "You are a Jew and I am a Samaritan woman. How can you ask me for a drink?" (For Jews do not associate with Samaritans.)

Jesus answered her, "If you knew the gift of God and who it is that asks you for a drink, you would have asked him and he would have given you living water."

"Sir," the woman said, "you have nothing to draw with and the well is deep. Where can you get this living water? Are you greater than our father Jacob, who gave us the well and drank from it himself, as did also his sons and his flocks and herds?"

Jesus answered, "Everyone who drinks this water will be thirsty again, but whoever drinks the water I give him will never thirst. Indeed, the water I give him will become in him a spring of water welling up to eternal life."

The woman said to him, "Sir, give me this water so that I won't get thirsty and have to keep coming here to draw water."

He told her, "Go, call your husband and come back."

"I have no husband," she replied.

Jesus said to her, "You are right when you say you have no husband. The fact is, you have had five husbands, and the man you now have is not your husband. What you have just said is quite true."

"Sir," the woman said, "I can see that you are a prophet. Our fathers worshiped on this mountain, but you Jews claim that the place where we must worship is in Jerusalem."

Jesus declared, "Believe me, woman, a time is coming when you will worship the Father neither on this mountain nor in Jerusalem. You Samaritans worship what you do not know; we worship what we do know, for salvation is from the Jews. Yet a time is coming and has now come when the true worshipers will worship the Father in spirit and truth, for they are the kind of worshipers the Father seeks. God is spirit, and his worshipers must worship in spirit and in truth."

The woman said, "I know that Messiah" (called Christ) "is coming. When he comes, he will explain everything to us."

Then Jesus declared, "I who speak to you am he."

The Woman at the Well

Jesus sits by Jacob's old well,
Soon a woman comes by;
When He asks for a drink of water
She can't imagine why.

For Jews and Samaritans didn't mix,
So, she could not conceive...
She would be the first of many...
Samaritans who'd believe.

She doesn't know who Jesus is,
For she's been living in sin;
How does He know all that she's done,
The what, the where, and when?

Jesus says, "I am the true Living Water,
And this well won't run dry."
She asks, "And where will I find this water?"
He says, "Don't you know...it is I?"

"Those who drink from Jacob's old well,
Will thirst just as before;
But those who drink Living Water,
Will never thirst anymore."

This woman's soul needed saving,
Jesus would pay for her sin;
He knew if she drank Living Water
Sin's battle she could win.

Just like for that sinful woman,
He'll meet you right where you are;
He'll come to live deep in your heart
Then He'll remove every scar.

When Jesus comes into your life,
He gives you a nature brand new,
He comes right in and then cleanses from sin,
And makes a new person of you.

Turn the Other Cheek

Friend, the world has been programmed to believe that if a person does something to you, that you have every right to do something back to them. Do you honestly believe that? I should hope not for the Lord has too many scriptures in the Bible that refute that statement. In fact, if you look at how Jesus lived His life, you will see that the opposite is true.

Jesus is the One who said to turn the other cheek; and the scriptures tell us that when He was reviled, He reviled not again (in other words He didn't revile back). The impressive thing to me is that He not only said to do these things but He never told us to do anything that He didn't do Himself. He always set the example for us, unlike so many today that have a tendency to tell their children, "Do as I say, not as I do."

I truly believe we can walk away feeling good about ourselves when we follow Jesus' example or we can walk away in defeat and regret when we don't follow that same example. The choice is ours my friend, what will yours be?

Read Matthew Chapter 5 and then focus on verse 39: But I say unto you, That ye resist not evil: but whosoever shall smite thee on thy right cheek, turn to him the other also.

Read Luke Chapter 6 and then focus on verse 29:And unto him that smiteth thee on the one cheek offer also the other; and him that taketh away thy cloak forbid not to take thy coat also.

Read I Corinthians Chapter 4 and then focus on verse 12: And labour, working with our own hands: being reviled, we bless; being persecuted, we suffer it

Read I Peter Chapter 2 and then focus on verse 29: Who, when he was reviled, reviled not again; when he suffered, he threatened not; but committed himself to him that judgeth righteously:

Turn the Other Cheek

It's hard to live in this cruel world -
To turn the other cheek,
But we must try if peace on earth
Is truly what we seek.

It seems to be much easier
To just retaliate,
As many do - who never stop
And think about their fate.

But Jesus turned the other cheek
Each time He was reviled,
And we should do the very same
If we are called His child.

There are times that we may suffer
Our soul may feel deep pain.
But if we'll turn the other cheek
Our joy will still remain.

Remember...

Jesus, when He was ridiculed
Never tried to repay,
He said, "Father, forgive." and then
Continued on His way.

We can find all sadness - sorrow
Even heartache and loss,
Traded for peace, love and joy by
Jesus' death on the cross.

And those who accept Him will find
They have a whole new life,
God's matchless grace soon replaces

289

All their sorrow and strife.
Once our soul meets the Savior we'll
Have the answers we seek,
And now if men try to hurt us
We can turn the other cheek.

It takes a real man to simply
Back off and walk away,
When the world says, "It's my right to
Turn around and repay."

It will never be easy to
Try and do the right thing,
But you'll find it's worth the effort
For God's blessings it'll bring.

Use Time Wisely

Dear One, how much time do we spend in front of the television set, how much time in front of the computer and reading worthless books and gossip magazines?

With so little free time on our hands how much time do we have to give to the Lord and His work? That should be our number one priority but instead we give God the leftovers. Really we should turn our lives around and live them in reverse. If we start to give the Lord more of our spare time; we'll find that it brings us so many blessings and so much happiness. The Lord gave us twenty-four hours in a day of life as a gift and along with it comes the responsibility to use the time wisely.

If we'll begin to use our own time in a profitable manner, it can have an incredible effect on those around us, starting with our children. And then it will become contagious and spread to others in our home, office, neighborhood, church and Bible Study.

Read Psalms Chapter 89 and then focus on verse 47: Remember how short my time is: wherefore hast thou made all men in vain?

Read Psalms Chapter 115 and then focus on verse 18: But we will bless the LORD from this time forth and for evermore. Praise the Lord.

Read Matthew Chapter 16 and then focus on verse 3: And in the morning, It will be foul weather to day: for the sky is red and lowering. O ye hypocrites, ye can discern the face of the sky; but can ye not discern the signs of the times?

Read Romans Chapter 13 and then focus on verse 11: And that, knowing the time, that now it is high time to awake out of sleep: for now is our salvation nearer than when we believed.

Read Colossians Chapter 4 and then focus on verse 5:

Walk in wisdom toward them that are without, redeeming the time

Read I Timothy Chapter 4 and then focus on verse 1: Now the Spirit speaketh expressly, that in the latter times some shall depart from the faith, giving heed to seducing spirits, and doctrines of devils;

Use Time Wisely

Lord, I need to use time wisely
But I know You can see;
There's so much confusion - that things...
Seem hard for one like me.

I come home from work and often
Turn on the television,
Then quickly turn it off for it's...
...Nothing but derision.

Only sadness and sorrow just...
Too much heartache and pain,
Take away meanness and violence...
Little else would remain.

Everywhere I turn I find
There's bad news all around...
Then I remember there's good news
And I know where it's found.

I can find it in Your Word, Dear Lord,
I need to read it more,
But since I tend to procrastinate...
I'm glad You don't keep score.

People don't learn much that helps them...
To live their daily life,
When watching television with...
Their husband or their wife.

What good can possibly come from
Watching man maim and kill?
One thing it can do for sure is...
Drive men crazier still.

So help us spend less of our time
In front of that T.V.
And more reading Your Word, Dear Lord,
Since that's how it should be.

We need to fill our minds with things,
To give us joy and peace.
Just as Your Word brings blessings that
For us will never cease.

So, let us start our children out
To wisely use their time,
Then when they grow up they won't
Waste theirs as I have mine.

Are You Afraid to Die?

The story "Are You Afraid to Die" was written one day when I was thinking about an episode that happened to my Momma when I was in my late twenties and had only known the Lord for a few years.

I was going over to my parents' home to pick up my momma for a late lunch. I started to call and tell her I was on my way, but decided since I was already running late that I'd just hurry on over. When I pulled up she was standing in the driveway with the next door neighbors. I thought perhaps they were just talking, but soon found out, that after a man broke in and tried to attack her, the Lord gave her protection and wisdom in her words; so, she was able to get out the door. Living on a major thoroughfare with lots of traffic, once she got outside she was able to run next door for help. They called 911 and the police came out, but never called to say that they caught the man.

God is so good and gave her angels of protection, the ability to keep calm and just the right words to say; all the while she had this stranger pawing all over her. He seemed to be drunk so we felt like that was why he let her wiggle away from his grasp, but of course ultimately we knew the Lord was her Protector and Provider.

I've also read and heard some amazing true stories of God's deliverance from what could have been dire circumstances, sometimes even life- threatening situations.

God is always with us, even in the most severe times of our lives and although things may not turn out the way we would want them to, He is right there with us, just as He was with Daniel in the lion's den and with Shadrach, Mishach and Abednigo in the fiery furnace.

Read Psalms Chapter 139 and then focus on verses 7-12 : Where can I go from your Spirit? Where can I flee from your presence? If I go up to the heavens, you are there; if I make my bed in the depths, [a] you are there. If I rise on the wings of the dawn, if I settle on the far side of the sea, even there your hand will guide me, your right hand will hold me fast. If I say, "Surely the darkness will hide me and the light become night around me," even the darkness will not be dark to you; the night will shine like the day for darkness is as light to you.

Are You Afraid to Die?

"Are you afraid to die?" the man in the ski-mask growled.

I was probably in shock and too amazed to be afraid. I believe I've heard something about adrenaline rushes. Only an hour ago I was sitting reading my Bible, having my morning devotions.

This isn't real; I must have forgotten to wake up this morning, because I know I'm dreaming, but I'm sure I'll wake up soon. I have to.

Suddenly I was jolted back to reality when the masked-man jerked me by the hair.

He said, "I repeat lady, are you afraid to die?"

I silently prayed for the Lord to give me the wisdom to know what to say to calm this man down. He seemed so frantic when he came up behind me and put his arm around my neck. Next thing I knew, he was forcefully leading me into the den and throwing me down on the couch.

The first words I remember uttering were, "I don't know why you're doing this, but there's one thing I do know and that is - God loves you more than you know!"

"Oh, my god, you mean I'z in the home of a Jesus Freak?"

I said, "I don't know what you mean by Jesus Freak. I doubt that people would call me a freak simply because I love the Lord. Yes, I read His Word and go to church, but that doesn't mean I'm some weirdo or fanatic. I didn't always have a relationship with the Lord myself, not until I was twenty-six did I really know what that meant."

The masked man sarcastically said, "I used to go to church when I was little."

And then in a little softer tone he said, " My grandma used to take me, cause I be livin' wit her. She done took me to church most every Sunday. But then when I was ten she went an' died. So I was put in a foster home. But dem peoples didn't want me; dey just wanted dat money dey gots ever month. But I rand away when I was fo'teen and I been livin' in duh streets from den till I be nineteen, den I met my girlfrin' and we been together ever since. We be livin' wit her mama cause we don't gots no money for our own place."

I began thinking to myself that this guy seemed to be calming down. What else could I say to work my way out of this dangerous, possibly fatal, situation?

I began to pray to myself, "Lord, give me Your wisdom, and send Your angels to help me. Please, put a hedge of angels around me and convince this man of his need to repent of the lifestyle he's been living . Help him to see the need to get his life right before You."

"My name is Debbie, what's your name?" I casually questioned.

"Oh, no ya don't. Ya think I'm just stupid don't ya? Well, I ain't that stupid! I ain't given ya no nothin'; besides ya ain't gonna be callin' nobody anyway." he said coldly; and in a way that gave me chills up and down my spine. I realized my palms were starting to sweat.

Lord, keep me calm and please, don't let me appear to be afraid.

"You know, years ago I was ready to take my life, I was in such a hopeless state. Out of the blue, a friend called and invited me to church one Saturday and, although I hadn't been a churchgoer, I told her I'd go. The very next morning I got myself and all three of my children up and ready to go. My ex-husband had me in tears before the kids and I managed to leave the house. I started not to go, but something pushed me out the door. Once I arrived, and the service started, I knew what I was hearing was the truth. The message I heard that day changed my life, and my future, forever."

"Well, what'd ya hear?" this man asked meekly.

"I heard that I can know for sure I'm going to heaven. And because God sent His Son, the Lord Jesus, to die on the cross to pay for my sins, and the sins of the entire world; now heaven's doors are open to me and to everyone else. All people have to do is believe: that Jesus was God's Son, that He was born, that He died on the cross for our sins, was buried and rose again on the third day just as it says in the Bible. If they truly believe these things; and they ask Jesus to come into their lives to be their Savior and Lord, they will be saved. Salvation is a free gift to everyone and all you have to do is accept the free gift. That's what I did years ago when I was twenty-six and it totally changed my life and the lives of all my family and friends. Have you done it too?" I asked the masked man casually.

"What difference do it make? I done so much bad that ain't no god gonna forgive me. It's too late fer me. In fact, Debbie, uh, lady, uh I broke in yur house here tonight cause I was gonna steal any money and jewelry I could find. If'n ya caused me any trouble I was plannin' to kill ya! I was gonna make ya drive yer car out to the country to uh place I knowz an' den blow ya brains outta yo head. 'So how kin God forgive me?'"he asked in a calmer, more serious tone.

"Nothing you've done is too hard for God to forgive. Jesus' death on the cross covered 'not just some sins, but all sins.' All you have to do is talk to God and tell Him, some thing like, 'Lord, I may not understand it all, but I do want to go to heaven when I die, and I 'believe You sent Your Son Jesus to die on the cross to pay for my sin, so that I can go to heaven and be with You someday.' I'm asking You, Jesus, to come into my life right now and be my Savior and Lord, and I thank You for dying for me, please help me to live for You. Forgive me for all my past sins for I know You died on the cross to pay for all those sins.' When you say those words, the Lord Jesus immediately comes to live in your heart. He'll be there for you from now on and He'll be your comforter, your guide, your healer, He'll be your everything. He'll even be your best friend, who will never leave you or forsake you.

If you've never done this why don't you do it right now? Don't wait for none of us ever knows what tomorrow will hold .We can't afford to put this off. If you'd like to do it I'll help you by saying the words and letting you say them after me and then you can thank Jesus for saving you in your own words. Would you like to do that now?"

I asked this now calmer and quieter young man.

"What do you have to lose," I continued.

"Well, I guess I ain't got nothin' to lose, cause I already done lost every thin' anyway. I just want Him to forgive me and I wants my girlfrin' to take me back. You think she will?" He meekly asked as he pulled his mask off, revealing a cleancut, nice looking young face.

"I know the Lord can mend broken lives and relationships and make all things new. I also know that He's a gentleman and He won't do anything without being asked, for He's not pushy. So you'll have to ask Him, and believe He is able and will do what He has promised." I said thoughtfully.

"Okay, I guess I'm ready den; and by the way, my name is Jeremy."

'Jeremy, repeat after me. Lord, I......."

And Jeremy closed his prayer by saying, "Lord, thank Ya for sendin' yer Son to die fer me and Jesus thank Ya for comin' down here and dyin' fer me so I kin be in heaven someday, Amen!"

'Jeremy, God has forgiven you and now forgive yourself.' Consider contacting those you have wronged in person, by phone or even by a letter; confess to them and ask them to forgive you. But whether you do that or not, it's very important to find a church to atttend. I have a Bible I'm going to give you, and I'm going to mark a lot of passages in it; and if you'll read them, it will help you grow in your relationship with the Lord. Pray daily, and if you ever need to talk, feel free to call me. You know Jeremy, your grandma is so happy to see this happening, for now she knows you'll be in heaven with her someday.

I forgive you for coming in my home today, and I'm going to let you leave quietly. I want you to take my phone number in case there's ever a need to call me. And by the way, to answer your question - Are you afraid to die?- Why should I be? There will be such great things waiting for me there. Besides, if my Father loved me enough to send His Son to die for me, and Jesus loved me enough to suffer and die on the cross; then I know they would never lie to me. And they say in the Word, 'Eye has not seen nor ear heard, neither has entered into the heart of man, the things that God has prepared for those who love Him.' To be honest with you I'm actually looking forward to it."

When Jeremy left my home, 'he was a new man in Christ, and I was freaked out!' I fell apart. I can't really say it was from fear, no, I would say more from

relief that I was still alive, and that the Lord had turned a frightening situation completely around; and to think that someone had just stepped from death into life anew. How could I be afraid to die?

I probably should have called the police but I have been praying for Jeremy for five years now . He calls me once every few months to let me know how well he's doing and what's going on at his church. He has a wonderful Christian girlfriend now and it looks like they'll be getting married soon.

'I never asked Jeremy what he had done, because I'll find out in heaven. He's not that man anymore, anyway. That man died one day five years ago.'

Hey! Miss Carolyn/No Butts About It

Dear One, this story is going to surprise you, but I decided to include it in the book for my hope is that it will bring a smile to your face and to your heart as well. It may seem a little crazy, but I decided to write a story from the point of view of our sofa in the family room, if the sofa could talk.

What would your furniture say if it could talk? Hopefully it would have a lot of great things to share about you and your family and the activities that take place in your home.

In this story, Fanstory is mentioned and it is a website where you can post your work to share with others. I posted some of my poems and stories on the site in hopes that it would bless someone or perhaps even lead someone to a saving knowledge of the Lord Jesus Christ.

I hope it makes you grin and giggle.

Read Proverbs Chapter 17 and then focus on verse 22: A merry heart doeth good like a medicine: but a broken spirit drieth the bones

Read Proverbs Chapter 15 and then focus on verse 13: A merry heart maketh a cheerful countenance: but by sorrow of the heart the spirit is broken.

Hey! Miss Carolyn/No Butts About It

Oh, hi and what is your name? Miss Priss; well, Miss Priss, it's awfully nice to meet you. I'm so excited about winning this fantastic prize. I can't wait to get started on the letter. I couldn't believe it when they told me I had been chosen to receive this special gift. I've been trying to imagine for quite some time what I would say to Miss Carolyn, if I was ever given the chance. Now that I have it, well, I didn't realize it would be so hard to let someone put my thoughts on paper.

Here goes.

Hey! Miss Carolyn, what an awesome opportunity I've been afforded and I just can't wait to get started. I've been awarded the chance to have a sternooooggrrrra...oh, well...the lady that came over to write down my surprise letter will know what word to put. Golly, I've never been given anything, much less something as unbelievable as this opportunity. Someone put my name, Sofamay, in a drawing for one of the...whatever-they-ares...to come over and let me dictate a letter to give to you, since I can't write it myself.

First, I would just like to say, it has been such a privilege to be in your home. If I could have chosen the location where I would be placed - and I knew then what I know now - I would have chosen to be with your family these last eight, wonderful years.

I have to admit, as your sofa I've seen a lot of use, especially since I make out into a bed. You have so many people over, some for a few hours and others for weeks, months or even a few for a year. I must say, it's always been so much fun. Of course, I usually see people from the bottom up, and as bottoms go I've seen all sizes, shapes and weights. Speaking of bottoms, isn't yours getting a little bigger than usual? Maybe it just seems like it. I could be mistaken, it's just that from my viewpoint...uh, oh well, forget it...I didn't mean to bring up a sore subject.

I'm not joking when I say I have loved being in your home, and I'm not complaining about anyone's bottom, for they've all been nice and warm and soft. Well, some of the men's butts seemed to be a little bit firmer. But all bottoms aside - oops! - I mean kidding - all kidding aside it's been great...

I've enjoyed holding up the likes of all of your friends, including Jim, the missionary, who comes four or five times a year for a week to a month each time. Have you noticed, even though he has his own bedroom here, he chooses to sleep on me many nights? And, that's okay I'm not complaining, in fact, I'm flattered. And when all your children and grandchildren come, I love listening to the kids talking with one another, after all the grown-ups have gone to bed. They are always so much fun and so sweet.

Remember the time all the ladies from the halfway house in Dallas came to visit? They rented a van and drove fourteen hours one way, because you said you were homesick and missed them. You thought, after moving to Georgia, you'd never see them again. Wow! You had fifteen ladies sleeping all over the house. I remember you crying when they arrived, I guess because you were so happy to see them, and when they were getting ready to leave you were bawling like a baby. They stayed a week and I thought you'd get enough of them; but you never get enough of anybody, do you? I have to say, I never had that much weight on me at one time before in all my sofa life.

I thought about the time when I was in your house in San Antonio. You had Bible Study there, and everybody brought food, which they never failed to spill on me. I enjoyed it, but after they left, I waited to hear you complain to Mr. Bill about the mess. You never did.

It's been a great life, and although your neighbor, Sharon, thinks you should get yourself a new couch, I was so happy to hear you tell her you didn't want one. It was great when I heard you say it would be impossible to find just my color again. I know I'm getting fairly old in couch-years and yet you put your new couch in the basement-den. I was so flattered. Miss Carolyn, I can't last forever and my time is probably drawing closer and closer, and when the time comes that I have to go, don't feel badly. I will always remember being in your home, for all the holidays and the happy times and the sad times, like when your Momma died and your Daddy died and your son-in-law, Jeff, died; you loved them so much. When your young niece Autumn died in the car wreck, it was especially sad; it was one week before her seventeenth birthday. And it was bad and sad enough when Emily and Bud died, although they were pretty old in dog years. I was so glad I could be a comfort for you and your family.

Having the people from prison come to live with you over the years has been a great experience; I've learned to love everyone's butt unconditionally, just like you're always telling everybody to do. In fact, now you tell all those people to do that when you're on that site thing, or whatever it is you do or go to on your computer. Fanstory! That's the name of it. I hope those people don't get tired of hearing about God all the time. You know I don't or I would have blown my cushions long ago.

Being with you and your family has been a blessing, as you say, and no butts about it. I wouldn't trade the years I've spent here for the opportunity to be in any other home, even if I had the chance. Seriously, your home has been my home and you've been so good to me, your butt's been mine, and the butts of all your family and friends, so I just want to say one more thing: there are no better butts in the world.

Oh, by the way I remember now--the word was stenographer.

Love from,

Sofamay

Santa and the Baby Jesus

"Santa and the Baby Jesus" is a short story that I wrote one year when it was just before Christmas. So many people think anything to do with Santa has to be wrong, but I wrote this little story for parents as well as children to read and perhaps realize there can be happy stories that can be read to our children, and they have a great lesson for them or a moral to the story.

I hope that you'll find this story totally different than any Christmas story you've ever read and that it will truly give you a blessing. I pray that it will be a blessing not only to you but to your children and grandchildren as well.

Even an old man called Santa Claus could and would be blessed by seeing the Son of God and having a life changing experience.

Read Luke Chapter 2 and then focus on verses 1-20 : In those days Caesar Augustus issued a decree that a census should be taken of the entire Roman world. This was the first census that took place while Quirinius was governor of Syria.) And everyone went to his own town to register.

So Joseph also went up from the town of Nazareth in Galilee to Judea, to Bethlehem the town of David, because he belonged to the house and line of David. He went there to register with Mary, who was pledged to be married to him and was expecting a child. While they were there, the time came for the baby to be born, and she gave birth to her firstborn, a son. She wrapped him in cloths and placed him in a manger, because there was no room for them in the inn.

And there were shepherds living out in the fields nearby, keeping watch over their flocks at night. An angel of the Lord appeared to them, and the glory of the Lord shone around them, and they were terrified. But the angel said to them, "Do not be afraid. I bring you good news of great joy that will be for all the people, in the town of David a Savior has been born to you; he is Christ[a] the Lord. This will be a sign to you: You will find a baby wrapped in cloths and lying in a manger."

Suddenly a great company of the heavenly host appeared with the angel, praising God and saying,

"Glory to God in the highest and on earth peace to men on whom his favor rests."

When the angels had left them and gone into heaven, the shepherds said to one another, "Let's go to Bethlehem and see this thing that has happened, which the Lord has told us about."

So they hurried off and found Mary and Joseph, and the baby, who was lying in the manger. When they had seen him, they spread the word concerning what had been told them about this child, and all who heard it were amazed at what the shepherds said to them. But Mary treasured up all these things and pondered them in her heart. The shepherds returned, glorifying and praising God for all the things they had heard and seen, which were just as they had been told.

Santa and the Baby Jesus

Santa Claus couldn't believe his eyes when he saw the tiny baby lying in the manger filled with hay. He couldn't imagine a baby, any baby, being born in a stable on such a cold winter's night. When he left the North Pole he would never have believed that he, the mere Santa Claus, would be seeing the Son of God on the very night that he was born. After he landed and he began to realize who these people really were, he suddenly felt overwhelmed with emotion at the thought of being in the presence of the Son of an all Holy and Righteous God.

Santa began to question in his mind, "Why had he been allowed to land here and what was he to do?"

He had always known that someday God was going to send His Son into the world, but he had no idea how, when or where this was going to take place.

He thought to himself, "What a privilege, I've been given." And he began to question, "Why have I received such a wonderful blessing? Seeing Baby Jesus and His parents lodging in a stable in the town of Bethlehem was the last thing I was expecting to see tonight."

He silently, in the quietness of his mind, began to talk to God the Father saying, "I don't understand why this has happened to me and I just want to run and hide, for I feel so unworthy, Lord, being in the presence of Your Son. I just keep thinking that, all these years I've tried to bless people especially little children and now I feel that everything I've done or ever will do is so insignificant, why bother. I feel like I'm nothing. Show me why You had me stop here. Please, Lord!"

Mary and Joseph could sense that Santa was feeling overwhelmed and made an effort to make him feel more comfortable and welcome. They said, "Santa, don't worry for you know that Jesus' Father loves you and He wouldn't want you to feel uncomfortable. He wants you to be happy, ecstatic, especially tonight! We have been given such a privilege and you have been called upon by God the Father, to take part in this awesome, spectacular, holy event."

Mary said, "Think about how I felt when God told me I was going to be His Son's mother. I felt pretty overwhelmed myself at first, after all, I was betrothed to Joseph and I began to worry about what people were going to think of us not being married. No one knew I was having the Son of God and no one would have believed it anyway. Almost immediately, I began to feel honored and closer to God the Father. I wanted to know what He had planned for me and I wanted even more to be obedient to Him for He knows what's best for us all."

Joseph then said, "Santa, how do you think it was for me? At first I didn't understand how my betrothed could have gotten pregnant. I was hurt and disappointed, that is until God the Father and Mary helped me understand it all.

In the beginning I was only worried about what everyone was going to say about Mary being pregnant and we were not even married yet. And would anyone believe that she was pregnant by God's Spirit?

I didn't know anything but that I loved and trusted God and Mary. So, Santa, don't feel badly or inferior for God the Father has a different job for each of us to do. The important thing is to find out what it is He has for us individually.

Personally, I think you've had a pretty important assignment given to you by our Father. Just think, if you weren't dedicated to the job that you've been given, millions of little children would be missing out on so much."

Mary said, "Rest here with us for a little while before you have to go on your way and tell us all about your travels."

Santa hesitantly told Mary and Joseph, "I think it's amazing that I've always delivered my gifts on December twenty- fifth and God chose to send His Son into the world on the same night. I always knew He was coming but it is so wonderful to know that from now on I'll be delivering my gifts to boys and girls in every land, because it's Jesus' birthday. No longer will December twenty-fifth be called Saint Nicholas Day, from now on the world will call it Christmas. It's the day that the Son of God, the Christ child was born."

Santa had always loved children from every country in the world. He tried very hard to make them all happy, especially those from the poorer nations. He knew they never had much to begin with and sometimes not even enough to eat. In fact, it nearly broke his heart, when he got to some of the children's homes and he saw the way they had to live.

It was hard for him not to cry for it made him very sad. He wished he could make things better for everyone and especially for the little children that were suffering so much and living in poverty.

When Baby Jesus moved His tiny arms a little bit, Santa asked, "Do you think I might be able to hold Baby Jesus for a few minutes before I have to take off? I would consider it such a blessing to know that, once upon a time, I held the Son of God Himself in my big old hands.

I always thought God gave me these large hands, because He knew I would need them to deliver all these presents. And some of the gifts are quite large and others are very heavy. I'll never forget that these same hands that deliver packages, got to hold the Son of Almighty God."

Mary handed the Babe wrapped in swaddling clothes to the jolly old gentleman. She knew he would be very careful with her Baby Boy and she had no reason to be afraid. After the long, hard trip she and Joseph had made and with her being pregnant, it had been a great relief to have an easy delivery.

She had been resting for a couple of hours when Santa arrived, so she had actually been able to enjoy talking with him; although she was beginning to feel a little bit tired after such a long, stressful day. It had taken them so long to find a place to stay, for every place they stopped was already full.

Mary and Joseph had no idea they wouldn't be able to find a room anywhere in Bethlehem, and that she would have to deliver her Baby lying in the hay on the floor of a stable.

As Mary gave birth, all the animals in the stable seemed to understand what was going on and apparently they knew that something very special was happening. They were all trying to get as close as they could to Mary and Joseph. It was as though they were all there, because they wanted to give her their moral support. In fact, it seemed as if the animals were suddenly talking back and forth to one another about what was happening.

After Santa had been holding Baby Jesus for quite a while, and Jesus had been quietly sleeping in his arms without making a sound, he knew he had to leave. It made his heart feel so heavy at the thought of leaving for he had never felt like this before in his very long life.

He was beginning to like this and feel very comfortable in the presence of God's Son and His family. It was as if, there were a magnet trying to keep him there, and he literally had to force himself to leave. He was definitely hoping to see this family year after year from now on for he already loved them very much.

Well, Santa knew he had to face the facts, it was getting late and he had lots and lots of deliveries to make before he could head back home to the North Pole and Mrs. Claus. He could already smell the wonderful meal she would, as always, have waiting on the table for him when he got there.

He was usually a little bit full from all the snacks the children had made for him. Sometimes it was cookies and milk, other times it was homemade fudge, a piece of cake or once in awhile it might even be a sandwich.

For some reason, he always felt like he was obligated to eat the goodies set out by the children. But somehow he never failed to be able to eat those nice, hot meals his beloved wife would have prepared for him, ready and waiting on the big old, wooden table.

Santa leaned over and kissed Baby Jesus on the forehead, then turned around and told Mary and Joseph, "God bless both of you and Baby Jesus and may you have many more wonderful Christmases to come. I'll be hoping to see you all next year wherever you're living."

Santa had no idea of what was ahead for this family, only God the Father knew what He had planned for Jesus, Mary and Joseph. But Santa knew the world would never be the same after this night and neither would he. From now on December twenty-fifth would be called Christmas in memory of Jesus' birthday and it would be celebrated all over the world.

Santa had to rush to catch up on his deliveries, after spending so much time with Baby Jesus and his parents over in Bethlehem. He was anxious to get home so he could tell Mrs. Claus all about this trip.

He really hoped that just by hearing what had taken place, she would be able to feel a little bit as blessed as he did. After deliveries each year, he would go back home and spend a couple of hours eating and relaxing. Mrs. Claus was always waiting for a full report of the highs and lows of his night's adventures.

Boy! He had a lot to tell his dear wife tonight. He couldn't remember having ever been this excited about what he had to tell on any of his past trips. But this one had been totally different than all the rest.

He had never, ever before and would never, ever again have another Christmas like this one. It almost grieved his heart that he'd had to leave Bethlehem but at least he was going to a fantastic home filled with people who loved him. He was already planning on how he could share the blessing of this night with his entire household.

As soon as the sleigh touched down, Santa got out and let some of the elves take the reindeer to their barn and feed them, after all they'd had a long, long hard journey. He then made a slow dash for the house where he knew Mrs. Claus was always waiting with a kiss, and with that wonderfully delicious, hot dinner. She always had everything laid out just perfectly on that big old table, ready for him to dive right in.

Santa tried his very best to relate every detail of his time spent in Bethlehem, exactly as it happened, for he wanted Mrs. Claus to be able to be half as filled with excitement and peace as he was. He spent quite a while going over every thing he could think of, and just relating the story made him weep with joy.

In fact, at times he was crying very hard and his nose was dripping so much he thought, "I'll bet my nose is going to look just like Rudolph's for the next week."

But after he told Mrs. Claus all his exciting news, at last he was finally ready to eat. She had put an awesome spread on the table. And of course, the elves had to have their Christmas feast too. They had worked very hard making toys all year. Santa had them join him at the table for he wanted to tell all the little people about his wonderful night. He didn't want to omit a single detail or they wouldn't get the full blessing from that Holy, Miraculous Night when Jesus Christ was born!

After finishing his luscious meal and relaxing a little while with Mrs. Claus, Santa headed for bed. He couldn't help thinking that he would be sound asleep before his head hit the pillow. But at first he couldn't stop wondering what Baby Jesus was going to do when he grew up. Then he also puzzled over what God the Father had planned for His wonderful Son to do with His life.

He asked himself, "Would He sit on a throne, would He wear a crown? Of course He would, for didn't every King wear a crown? Besides, he thought he had heard or read somewhere that Jesus would be called the King of the Jews."

Little did he know that Jesus would do both of those things in heaven; but first He would be beaten and abused, suffer and die on a cross, all because of His and the Father's unconditional love for all mankind.

Santa never realized that Jesus was born to be the greatest gift ever given - God's gift to us. He gave us the greatest gift ever given - He gave us the gift of salvation. Jesus bought and paid for the gift with His life, and wants to give it to every living human being.

What would Santa have done, if he had known in reality what he was privileged to have experienced?

I believe things would be a little bit different today. Maybe Santa would be leaving something besides toys for children. Perhaps the world would be a totally different place had he known what was coming and how serious the future events were going to be. Possibly Santa wouldn't even be delivering gifts on Christmas anymore, maybe he would have decided to deliver Jesus' gifts to the world. Maybe he would have become a pastor or an evangelist.

Who knows? But he didn't know anything about what the future held for Jesus and so we're still celebrating and Santa's still delivering packages on December twenty-fifth. So, boys and girls take advantage of the present situation: be thankful for the packages Santa brings you, accept the gifts that Jesus has for you, and then don't forget to thank God the Father for all your blessings.

God Bless You and Merry Christmas Everyone!

Was It an Angel?

We had been living in San Antonio for about a year when I needed to renew my Chaplaincy License in order to continue teaching a weekly Bible Study at the City Jail. They were offering the course at a local prison about ten miles out of town; and after finishing the course I was about a half mile down the road, headed home, when I passed an elderly man riding a bicycle. I thought to myself that he must be a little chilly, for it was quite cool out that day, and being out in the middle of nowhere made it seem so desolate. It was late in the day and the sun was starting to go down, and I was looking forward to getting home and starting supper.

As I reached the intersection and stopped at the blinking light, I heard, in what seemed like an audible voice, "The little man you passed needs help; now, go back and take him any money you have in your purse." I must admit I hesitated for a minute for I was anxious to get home, but I turned the car around in the middle of the intersection and then turned around again to pull up beside the little man I had passed. As I put the passenger window down, I said in Spanish, "Hola" and just started to hand him the twenty dollars I had collected out of my purse. When he saw the money, in broken English he said, "No, me have a jobby."

He proceeded to point to a plant nursery way off in the distance. I found out he rode his bicycle 8 miles one way to work each day and he was on his way home. He didn't want to take the money, but I told him in Spanish that he had to take it for the Lord wanted him to have it. He hesitantly took the twenty dollars and I told him, "God loves you and God bless you". I waved goodbye as I slowly pulled away.

As I drove home I thought about the man and how so many people won't even work at all and this man had been riding a bike to his job every day for years. rain or shine, no matter what the weather happened to be. And then I wondered if perhaps the little man was an angel that the Lord sent to bless my day.

Read Hebrews Chapter 13 and then focus on verses 1-3: Let brotherly love continue. Be not forgetful to entertain strangers: for thereby some have entertained angels unawares. Remember them that are in bonds, as bound with them; and them which suffer adversity, as being yourselves also in the body.

Was It an Angel?

One day I was driving my car
Out on the edge of town,
I passed a man riding his bike
No one else was around.

Wind was blowing and it was cold
I passed the man on by;
But before I reached the stop sign,
I heard a voice cry,

"That little man you passed needs help,
So turn around and go;
Give him the money in your purse
And don't make a big show."

I suddenly thought to myself,
"They always want money.
Guess I'll do what my Father says,
But this is not funny."

I found a twenty in my wallet,
Thought, "I'll drive up close as I can."
I put the window down and said "Hola"
Tried to hand the money to the man.

The little man said, "Me have jobby"
Pointed at a plant three miles away.
I said,"Yes, but you must take this,
The Lord wants to give you twenty dollars today."

He said, "Thank you" in broken English,
I thought I saw a tear in his eye.
Before I put the window up I told him,
"God loves you, God Bless you, and good bye."

While driving home I thought of him,
Rode a bicycle 8 miles to work.
Some won't start their car for a job,
That's probably why they're often called a jerk.

I drove farther on and wondered,
Could the little man I got to meet;
Be one of God's sweet, holy angels,
Riding his bicycle up and down the street?

The Master Painter

Dear One, have you ever thought about the beauty all around us, the awesome array of colors and the way they're blended and shaded just perfectly. The many beautiful colors in everything that exists, for all that has been created from animals, insects, plants, the earth, the planets. sky, oceans and seas, fish, birds, people and all the material things we have at our disposal.

I can just picture our wonderful, omnipotent, omniscient, omnipresent God, creating the whole thing. Can't you imagine His delight at the completion of each thing that He created? What a fantastic picture it would make, to paint the Lord Himself creating all of creation in its perfection. And to think He did it all just for us and for our enjoyment.

We may like to bless our children but our Father really went above and beyond for us. Not only the colors but the size and shapes of everything and each thing has its own special place to exist. We have so much to be thankful for and so many special blessings created exclusively for us.

We should thank and praise our Father for all Eternity, for all that He has done for us, but above all for His unconditional love, unending mercy and limitless grace. Just to think of what all He's done for us should make us shout with joy! Hallelujah!

Read Genesis All of Chapter 1:

In the beginning God created the heavens and the earth.

Now the earth was formless and empty, darkness was over the surface of the deep, and the Spirit of God was hovering over the waters.

And God said, "Let there be light," and there was light. God saw that the light was good, and He separated the light from the darkness. God called the light "day," and the darkness he called "night." And there was evening, and there was morning—the first day.

And God said, "Let there be an expanse between the waters to separate water from water." So God made the expanse and separated the water under the expanse from the water above it. And it was so. 8 God called the expanse "sky." And there was evening, and there was morning—the second day.

And God said, "Let the water under the sky be gathered to one place, and let dry ground appear." And it was so. God called the dry ground "land," and the gathered waters he called "seas." And God saw that it was good.

Then God said, "Let the land produce vegetation: seed-bearing plants and trees on the land that bear fruit with seed in it, according to their various kinds." And it was so. The land produced vegetation: plants bearing seed according to their kinds and trees bearing fruit with seed in it according to their kinds. And God saw that it was good. And there was evening, and there was morning—the third day.

And God said, "Let there be lights in the expanse of the sky to separate the day from the night, and let them serve as signs to mark seasons and days and years, and let them be lights in the expanse of the sky to give light on the earth." And it was so. God made two great lights—the greater light to govern the day and the lesser light to govern the night. He also made the stars. God set them in the expanse of the sky to give light on the earth, to govern the day and the night, and to separate light from darkness. And God saw that it was good. And there was evening, and there was morning—the fourth day.

And God said, "Let the water teem with living creatures, and let birds fly above the earth across the expanse of the sky." So God created the great creatures of the sea and every living and moving thing with which the water teems, according to their kinds, and every winged bird according to its kind. And God saw that it was good. God blessed them and said, "Be fruitful and increase in number and fill the water in the seas, and let the birds increase on the earth." And there was evening, and there was morning—the fifth day.

And God said, "Let the land produce living creatures according to their kinds: livestock, creatures that move along the ground, and wild animals, each according to its kind." And it was so. God made the wild animals according to their kinds, the livestock according to their kinds, and all the creatures that move along the ground according to their kinds. And God saw that it was good.

Then God said, "Let us make man in our image, in our likeness, and let them rule over the fish of the sea and the birds of the air, over the livestock, over all the earth, and over all the creatures that move along the ground."

So God created man in his own image in the image of God he created him; male and female he created them. God blessed them and said to them, "Be fruitful and increase in number; fill the earth and subdue it. Rule over the fish of the sea and the birds of the air and over every living creature that moves on the ground."

Then God said, "I give you every seed-bearing plant on the face of the whole earth and every tree that has fruit with seed in it. They will be yours for food. And to all the beasts of the earth and all the birds of the air and all the creatures that move on the ground—everything that has the breath of life in it—I give every green plant for food." And it was so. God saw all that he had made, and it was very good. And there was evening, and there was morning—the sixth day.

The Master Painter

It just seems so amazing that
From black and green and brown,
The Lord can paint a tree and then
He'll plant it in the ground.

With blue and white He paints the sky,
But sometimes black and gray,
When instead of sunshine
He paints a cloudy day.

Sometimes after the wind and rain,
He'll paint blue, green and red:
A beautiful reminder that
There's sunshine just ahead.

The evening skies of pink with
A little tint of peach;
Blending colors for all the shells
We find along the beach..

His flowers of many colors
Are painted Spring and Fall;
As a symphony of beauty
Enjoyed by one and all.

He paints red in the Robin's breast
And blue in every Jay.
How many colors in the Peacock's tail?
Only He can say.

The Master uses His brush to paint,
According to His will;
Until at last He calls us home,
He'll keep on painting still.

Until the end of time He'll paint,
He paints to hide our sin;
Red on black turns purest white when
Stirred in the hearts of men.

The red the blood, the black our sin,
The white So Great Salvation;
Painted by God's precious Son,
For every tribe and nation.

God the Father makes His art
Available to all;
Is there a painting by the Master
Adorning your heart's wall?

Was It By Accident?

Dear One, this short story was written as a means of encouraging others not to ever give up, but to remember God is always working behind the scenes. Even when we don't feel His presence He is there.

God is going to accomplish His plan for your life and it will be the best plan, but this only takes place with your permission for He's a gentleman and He's not going to violate your free will.

Friend, surrender your will to the one who loves you and knows and wants what is best for you. Often we think we know what's best but the One who created us is the only One who really knows. What we think we need may not be bad, but why settle for second best.

Nothing is ever by accident for a child of God who is walking with the Lord. And everything that happens in a believer's life is working together for good if they love the Lord and are called according to His purpose.

Don't miss out on all your blessings.

Read Ephesians Chapter 2 and focus on verses 4-10: But because of his great love for us, God, who is rich in mercy, made us alive with Christ even when we were dead in transgressions—it is by grace you have been saved. God raised us up with Christ and seated us with him in the heavenly realms in Christ Jesus, In order that in the coming ages he might show the incomparable riches of his grace, expressed in his kindness to us in Christ Jesus. For it is by grace you have been saved, through faith—and this not from yourselves, it is the gift of God— not by works, so that no one can boast. For we are God's workmanship, created in Christ Jesus to do good works, which God prepared in advance for us to do.

Was It By Accident?

The hot summer sun beat down on Bobby as he walked dejectedly, alone, head-held-down, from the baseball field. The game was over, and his team lost again. Most twelve-year-old boys in Houston, Texas in the l970's had some type of special plans with family or friends on a sunny, summer Saturday afternoon, but both Bobby's parents worked weekends. Bobby had not lived in Houston long enough to make any real friends. The other guys on his team, the Warriors, rooted for him when he was at bat and cheered him on when he made a hit or a run, but as soon as the game was over, they all seemed to disappear with their "old buds". He hoped that after the new school year started, maybe he'd be able to make some new friends.

Bobby noticed the thick coating of dust that gathered on his shoes and legs as he walked along the road to the little frame house his parents rented from Mr. Wilson. He wished his momma and daddy would be home when he got there. Since his daddy had just gotten a job, after being out of work for six weeks, he knew they would both be working until sometime after seven o'clock. They were always too tired to do anything when they got home, so that meant he'd be watching television the rest of the day - and this evening - until bedtime. There weren't any neighborhood kids to play with way out where they lived. He walked a mile and a half to practice and games, not only because he loved baseball, but also, to have some contact with other boys his age during the summer while school was out.

Today, the road was really dusty, for there had been no rain for the last four or five weeks. Every time a car passed him, it sent up a cloud of dust in his face, so he would try to cover his eyes with his hands or by pulling up his baseball shirt over his head. Just after the last car passed him, as he pulled up his shirt, he thought he saw something fly out of one of the car windows, so, as he lowered his own self-invented face-mask, he started looking around for something white. Over on the shoulder of the road, in a patch of weeds, he saw what appeared to be a post card. As he leaned over to pick it up, silently, he wondered why he was bothering to pick up a silly old post card, but maybe, it would have a picture of some far away, exotic land, and he could imagine himself there on a vacation with his parents. After all, it never hurt to dream, for he knew that was all it would ever be.

When he picked up the dusty card, before he turned it over, he noticed it was already addressed, and it even had a stamp on it. Maybe, he should put it in the mailbox at his house, so the postman could pick it up tomorrow. After all, the people in that big green convertible probably planned on mailing it.

When Bobby looked at the back of the card, it read, "Please, let me pray for you, if you have any needs or wants, please, list them on this card and put it in the nearest mailbox. And if you don't know for sure, that you're going to heaven when you die, I'll be glad to write you back and tell you how you can know that for sure."He was a little bit startled when he finished reading, and he almost threw the card back down on the ground, but instead, he casually put it in his pocket.

By the time he reached his house, Bobby was hot, hungry and thirsty, after all he had played nine innings, hit two runs in and walked a total of three miles. He was definitely ready for the huge peanut butter and jelly sandwich and ice-cold glass of Kool-Aid his momma had made, and left for him that morning before she went to work. He idly walked over and turned on the old black and white television set - his parents first purchase after they got married.

Bobby watched all his favorite Saturday afternoon and evening programs, had supper with Mom and Dad, took a much-needed bath and was ready to get into bed. Suddenly, he remembered the white card in the pocket of his baseball shirt, now on the floor in the washroom. He quietly got out of bed and tiptoed down the hall to the cubicle where his mother kept the dirty clothes until she had time to wash them. He picked through the stack and found his shirt with the card still in its pocket. He took the card back to his bedroom and reread the words once more,

"Please, let me pray for you."

And he couldn't help wondering, "Am I going to heaven when I die?"

He opened the drawer of his nightstand, pulled out his pen and began to write on the card. Before he knew it, he had totally covered the surface of the card with things he wanted to see happen in life. He asked for prayer for his family, that his momma and daddy wouldn't have to work so much and so hard, and for his friends back in Jacksonville, he hoped he would get to see them again someday. He hoped, he would go to heaven, since he had always said his prayers and at times he even felt he wanted to be a preacher or maybe a missionary somewhere way off in a foreign country. In fact, it might be in Africa, where he would live in a tent and see all the animals in the jungles. For some reason, he couldn't wait to get up in the morning and mail that card, although he wondered why, for he knew with the little money his parents had, he would probably never leave this little suburb of Houston, Texas. Besides, this whole thing with the card was probably some kind of a joke.

Bobby had no idea, that a very godly spinster who lived in England and owned a huge import-export business there, would soon have a life changing impact on his life right here in Houston. This dear lady felt led by the Spirit to win souls for the kingdom of God, and after a time of much prayer she decided to have cards printed and then bundled up and brought to one of her business locations. She enlisted many of her employees to help put cards into every one of the containers that left the plant. Then every order that was shipped out would have a white card in it with some life-changing questions and information on it. All over the world as people opened crates, boxes and cartons they would find their card.

Well, the family that passed Bobby on the road, that hot summer day, had always purchased a lot of things from England, through an import-export business and they had left the box from their latest purchase open in the back seat of their convertible. When they removed the expensive new camera from its nest of packing materials they failed to notice the little white card tucked inside. With the top down, at God's appointed time, the wind picked up the card and placed it in just the right spot along the road and at just the right time.

Each card was assigned a code number, so that if and when it was sent back, Miss Lively would know what box it had been in and where it had been shipped. Any cards that were returned, she had them divided up among a large group of volunteer prayer partners in her church. Each prayer partner prayed for all the requests at the Wednesday night prayer meeting and at home throughout the week.

The Hinson family didn't know anything about what had happened and what the future held, but they enjoyed their new camera immensely.

Pastor Robert Emmett, gave a wonderful message that Sunday in Atlanta, Georgia. At the end of the service, he said, "There's a very special couple in our congregation today and I'd like to ask them to come up and say a few words. Mr. and Mrs. Hinson, please, come and join me."

The pastor told his congregation, "Today, instead of the usual verse by verse bible teaching I always teach from the scriptures, I told you this true story because it is such a perfect example of what I want everyone to know. We all have divine appointments, and many times, our disappointments are God's divine appointments. What may seem alarming or disheartening today, is working together for good in our lives, and our Father will show us somewhere down the road, why He allowed that particular thing to take place. Many times, as I walked the dusty road home, I felt sorry for myself, and yet, it had to be, in order for me to become the person God the Father wanted me to be.

Friends, the card I picked up on that dusty road back in Texas so many years ago, was meant for this family. When they were contacted regarding the card and its contents, for remember Miss Lively thought they sent the card back, they decided to contact me and my family, and so did Miss Lively. Some years ago, Miss Lively went to be with the Lord, but the Hinsons, have kept in touch with me all these years. After reading my prayer requests they decided to be used by God to answer some of those petitions. They paid my way to college and then to seminary.

I used to picture God blowing softly on that open container and then with one more puff blowing that little white card to just the right place at just the right time.

Was it an accident? I don't think so, what about you?"

Bobby said, "Let's all give the Hinsons a warm Atlanta welcome!"

Heaven's Most Wonderful Daddy

Dear Friend, I wasn't going to include this poem in my book, for I omitted it from the first one. I felt perhaps it was too personal. I wrote this for my Daddy on His eightieth birthday and then read it at his funeral a little over a year later.

Although Daddy was my stepfather he had to have been hand-picked for us by the Lord, for he was such a true blessing; and life would have been a living hell if we had been raised by our real father. His second family truly suffered for their being his wife and children and my heart grieved for them. He may have had everything money could buy but he was an extremely cruel person.

When a dear friend read this poem, she recommended I add it this time for she felt it would bless someone, although she had no relationship with her Father and reading this poem made her a little sad. If that is your situation, please, look at this poem in the aspect of the Lord is your Daddy; for truly He is the real Daddy of us all. It's as if our earthly Father is a stepfather, whether they are the world's definition of a real or stepfather.

I pray that you have a wonderful real or step (earthly) Daddy but remember, either way, you have the greatest Daddy in the universe. I call Him Father God, you may call Him Lord, or simply God or by any of His many biblical names but whatever you call Him above all He's your loving heavenly Father (Daddy).

Praise His Name Forever!

Read Psalms Chapter 27 and then focus on verse 10: Though my father and mother forsake me, the Lord will receive me.

Read Exodus Chapter 20 and then focus on verse 12 : Honor your father and your mother, so that you may live long in the land the Lord your God is giving you.

Heaven's Most Wonderful Daddy

Daddy, I'm so glad Momma chose
You to be my Father,
And when you found she had me - you
Didn't say, "Why bother?"

God's plans are perfect and I'm glad
In mine he included you,
When Momma said, "I do!" - quickly
I said,"I do, too!"

I'm glad you loved Momma enough
To take us on - all three,
Many men would've said, "No, way!"
To Momma, Robby and me.

Each year I love you more and think
About how blessed I've been,
For the Lord, chose you as my Daddy
From among all other men.

You gave us all we ever needed
Thank God, He gave us you;
Even the things we wanted you tried
Your best to give those too.

Though you may not be rewarded
While living on this earth,
Your rewards up in Heaven
Are of far greater worth.

What can I say for all you've done
Mere words could ne'er express,
So I'll simply say,"I love you."
Nothing more - nothing less.

I don't get to see you enough -
We live so far away,
But in heav'n we'll all be together
For forever and a day.

I'm so glad the Lord gave me the
World's most wonderful Dad,
To think of a life without you
Always makes me sad.

If you get to heav'n before me,
I'll be there very soon,
Wait for me at the gates of Glory just
Beyond the sun and moon.

When I get there I'll tell all those
That I can possibly find,
Of all the good Daddy's in Heaven
The very best one is mine.

Happy Halloween

Dear One, many Christians refuse to participate in Halloween, due to the fact that they consider it to be a pagan holiday. I can understand their concern. Personally, our family uses the holiday to give out Christian tracts that young people will enjoy reading. We also like to give each child a bunch of goodies, because we want them to look forward to coming back to our house next year.

We must not limit the Lord, for He is able to use so many things for His glory. It's up to us to be available at all times for Him to use us. We need to be thankful for every opportunity we're given to serve Him, and willingly die to self and surrender completely to His will. The Lord is so thoughtful and such a gentleman that He will not violate our freewill, so it is imperative that we (and I want to emphasize) willingly allow Him to fill us with His Spirit in order to accomplish His purpose and plan through us.

So, friends, look for every time, date, occasion or holiday of any kind, that you might be able to turn into an opportunity for ministering or witnessing to others. It will bless you so, that soon you'll find yourself much more in tune to the Holy Spirit's leading. Next thing you know, you'll actually be seeking out those opportunities more and more, as you experience the blessings of the Lord, that only come with our obedience.

This year use Halloween to be a blessing, and if you have children you might either have a party for them at your home or church, (and dress them as Bible characters), or go with them as they go house to house. At each door have them say, "Happy Halloween!" instead of Trick or Treat, for that has a negative connotation. You might think about simply handing a tract to the person who is passing out the candy and say, "God bless you this evening!" You could be surprised by the reactions you'll receive.

From now on, enjoy Halloween!

Read Romans chapter 14 and then focus on verses 5-8: One man considers one day more sacred than another; another man considers every day alike. Each one should be fully convinced in his own mind. He who regards one day as special, does so to the Lord. He who eats meat, eats to the Lord, for he gives thanks to God; and he who abstains, does so to the Lord and gives thanks to God. For none of us lives to himself alone and none of us dies to himself alone. If we live, we live to the Lord; and if we die, we die to the Lord. So, whether we live or die, we belong to the Lord.

Happy Halloween

Witches, goblins and ghosts, oh no!
Lurk in the mist and smoke.
They hope to scare some little child,
To whom it's not a joke.

As they scare little boys and girls
It's innocents they rob,
And stealing little children's joy,
That's their favorite job.

Every child belongs to Jesus,
He watches o'er each one.
So, now witches, goblins and ghosts,
Aren't having any fun.

Since God has His mighty angels,
Their fiercest enemies;
They've almost lost their position
As scary entities.

They've become very limited
In what they say and do;
Now, Halloween's just not the same
As 'twas for me and you.

The children won't wear a scary
Mask or a strange costume.
Some will dress as little angels
And devils meet their doom.

Each one instead of saying boo
When someone answers the door,
They'll say,"Happy Halloween,
And many, many more!"

Wait!

Friend, do you have a problem running ahead of the Lord? I must say it is quite easy to do and yet it never pays off very well. I have always been little bit impatient when having to wait on anything, although before I knew the Lord I was much more impatient than I am now.

The difference, for example, is that I used to dread waiting in the line at the grocery story, until I found out the Lord would give me openings to witness to people in those very lines that I had once despised. Over the years, I have been given the opportunity to invite several people in to church or to a Bible Study in my home where they found the Lord, and then their families came and accepted Jesus as well; all due to being stuck in a line and the Lord opening the door for a conversation to begin.

Nothing is more of a blessing than having the opportunity to see souls saved and lives changed and the process can begin while you're waiting in a line somewhere. You just need to hear the Spirit and heed the call. I always think back about the first time it happened to me; and how I hesitated. I used to be very introverted and I didn't want to make a fool of myself, but the Lord let me know, if I would surrender, He'd do the talking for me, by putting His words in my mouth. Soon, Father God also delivered me from being an introvert, and turned me into a semi-extrovert! He also let me know being a fool for the Lord is a blast!

There have been times waiting impatiently, then getting tired of it, thus running ahead of my Father, has cost me dearly. Trying to hurry up for we want to see something happen now, never pays, for our Father's timing is perfect. If we get disappointed because we think our prayer is not being answered, we must remember He has a reason, and our disappointments are His divine appointments.

Read Psalms chapter 27 and then focus on verse 14: Wait on the Lord: be of good courage, and he shall strengthen thine heart: wait, I say, on the Lord.

Read Psalms chapter 33 and then focus on verse 20: Our soul waiteth for the Lord: he is our help and our shield.

Read Psalms chapter 37 and then focus on verse 7: Rest in the Lord, and wait patiently for him: fret not thyself because of him who prospereth in his way, because of the man who bringeth wicked devices to pass.

Read Isaiah chapter 40 and then focus on verse 31: But they that wait upon the Lord shall renew their strength; they shall mount up with wings as eagles; they shall run, and not be weary; and they shall walk, and not faint.

Wait!

Lord,
There are those times, that I don't know
Just what I am to do;
And I find it very hard to
Be still and wait on You.

All those times that I've run ahead
Things seemed to turn out wrong;
So help me learn to wait on You and
To stay where I belong.

I've always found it difficult
To simply sit and wait;
I guess I'm so impatient that
I feel I'm running late.

Things always do go better when
I rest and wait on You,
And when at last You choose to speak
I know Your words are true.

Waiting seems to be so boring
I want to break and run;
I feel like I'm just wasting time,
And missing all the fun.

In my heart I know I need to
Stop and smell the roses;
Give You time to part the waters,
Just as You did for Moses.

From now on I'm going to try
To leave things in Your hands;
To wait, pray, let You work and to
Ignore the world's demands.

But if I start to run ahead
Then, please, just holler. "Wait!"
I will stop right where I am and
I'll never hesitate.

In fact, when I think about it
Wondering what You'll do;
I believe it might be nice to
Be still and wait on You.

My Friend, Joann

The poem "My Friend, Joann" is included in this book not only for her recognition, but I want everyone to know what a blessing it is to have a relationship based on a foundation that lasts. And, the friendship that we have was given to us by our Father. We met at a prison weekend in Marlin, Texas about fifteen years ago and we'll be friends for Eternity. God is so good, and one of the greatest blessings He gives us is our friends.

There is no greater joy than serving the Lord with a friend. My prayer for you is that you'll have a relationship with someone like I have with Joann; and if you don't please, ask your heavenly Father, to bring you that special person. Ask Him to personally pick out your Eternal Sister in the Lord. You'll never regret it and when we see each other in heaven you can tell me all about the fun you've had together.

Thank you Father, for my friend Joann.

Read Proverbs chapter 17 and then focus on verse 17: A friend loveth at all times, and a brother is born for adversity.

Read John chapter 15 and then focus on verse 13: Greater love hath no man than this, that a man lay down his life for his friends

This verse from John may mean literally laying down or giving your life for a friend, or it can also mean giving your time and energy to meet the needs of a friend.

My Friend, Joann

The Lord gave me a good, good friend
About twelve years ago;
We don't live close together now,
But we're still on the go.

We have so much in common and
In some ways we're the same;
We both love guards and prisoners
Their souls our only aim.

We both like wearing make up and
We both have bright red hair,
When we head for prison - it's as
If we could walk on air.

We fly around the country - to
Prisons all over this sod,
Offering inmates a chance -
To put their faith in God.

They may spend their life in prison
God loves them just the same,
And they can have eternal life - if -
They call upon His name.

We let them know God loves them all
Unconditionally,
And their lives can now forever -
Change positionally.

Yes, it's true - not all will change
But there are those who will,
Only God knows who they are - He's
The One who paid their bill.

My friend and I will keep going - to
Prisons throughout the land.
Until the Lord takes us home to
Play in the angel band.

There's never a time when I'm down
That I won't hear the phone,
It's always the Lord through Joanne
Saying,"Cheer up, you're not alone!"

Joanne is the sister I didn't -
Have as I grew up
But oh, the joy and blessing since
The Lord has filled my cup.

He filled my cup with happiness
And joy I never knew,
When He gave me a special friend
And - Joanne, that friend is you.

Soldier

Dear Ones, this poem "Soldier" was written for all hose who have served our country in wartime and in peace, but especially those who served in Vietnam, Desert Storm and Iraq. They deserve our prayers, thanks and respect.

I wrote this poem when many were calling for us to bring our troops home and yet our fighting men felt they were doing the right thing helping people in these foreign lands that had no one to help them. My Son and Grandsons served and totally agreed with our president and their superiors that we needed to be there.

It's a hurtful thing to hear people in your own country condemning you for risking your life for our safety and protection, as well as trying to make things better for those in need.

We also need to pray for our enemies to find Christ for that's the only thing that will change their hearts.

Please read John Chapter 15 and then focus on verses 12-14: This is my commandment, That ye love one another, as I have loved you. Greater love hath no man than this, that a man lay down his life for his friends. Ye are my friends, if ye do whatsoever I command you

Read I Thessalonians chapter 1 and then focus on verses 2-3: We always thank God for all of you, mentioning you in our prayers. We continually remember before our God and Father your work produced by faith, your labor prompted by love, and your endurance inspired by hope in our Lord Jesus Christ.

Soldier

We love and appreciate you
For all that you have done,
While we sit here at home - laughing
And having so much fun.

Yes, you are far away from home
Fighting in a foreign land,
For many who are crying out
Return! They do demand.

You're fighting because you love this
Wonderful land of ours,
In fact when you were here at home,
You talked of her for hours.

There are those who'd rather let the
Enemy come to us,
If I was not a Christian - it
Might even make me cuss.

For I know you're doing what you
Always believed was right,
And remember those who love you
Still pray throughout the night.

Those in my family who are
So very far away,
They risk their lives for the ones who,
Say, "Leave, come home today!"

Soldiers, I pray God will keep His
Angels surrounding you ,
And I pray that in the end -
You'll make it safely through.

When the bullets are whizzing by
And bombs drop on the land
Don't forget the Lord will hold you
In the palm of his hand,

Until the time is right for you
To leave that fighting place,
May the Lord keep you safe by
His amazing grace.

Made in the USA
Charleston, SC
09 January 2015